APM Introduction to Programme Management

APM Introduction to Programme Management

Second edition

Association for Project Management

Association for Project Management
Ibis House, Regent Park
Summerleys Road, Princes Risborough
Buckinghamshire
HP27 9LE

British Library Cataloguing in Publication Data is available.
Paperback ISBN: 978-1-903494-58-5
eISBN: 978-1-903494-59-2

Cover design by Fountainhead Creative Consultants
Typeset by RefineCatch Limited, Bungay, Suffolk
in 11/14 Foundary Sans

Contents

Figures and tables

Figures

Tables

Foreword

Nearly a decade ago, APM published *APM Introduction to Programme Management*. At that time I had just been appointed Chair of the Olympic Delivery Authority charged with delivering the London Olympics 2012: the question on many people's lips was "Does Britain have what it takes to deliver such an ambitious programme given the perception of performance on major public sector programmes?" The answer is one more notch in the history of achievements that this country can lay claim to.

The field of programme and project management is both as old as time itself and also a young profession. When I started my career, project management was 'just a part of' whatever profession you happened to be in – too often with inglorious consequences for delivery that have lodged in the perceptions of many. Times have changed and now professionalism in project management has made successful delivery the expected norm. Recognition that programme management is much more than 'just big project management' is a relatively recent concept. The success of the London 2012 Olympics, and the 'Learning Legacy' shared with the world, has stimulated interest and progress in this field, most recently exemplified on Crossrail. These programmes are not so much a pinnacle of success as the beginning of the greatest proposed investment in infrastructure ever seen in this country. The National Infrastructure Plan sees a forward portfolio of work that will challenge our global skills to deliver – a challenge we must rise to if we are to achieve the growth and prosperity we owe to those who follow us.

While my career has been predominantly in infrastructure, the world of programme management stretches way beyond these limiting boundaries. Wherever change is required to deliver benefits to an organisation or society, there you will find a demand for programme management skills to realise the outcomes sought rather than simply deliver constituent project outputs that do not quite achieve expectations. One can see, in the worlds of IT and defence, examples beyond infrastructure of both success and failure at programme level that build on successful project delivery.

This update to *APM Introduction to Programme Management* brings new insights as to what programme management is all about. It is an 'easy read' for the top executives, for those relatively new to programme management who have a thirst for knowledge and for the project management community who should, and need to, understand how their project management skills play into the 'bigger picture'. To all of you, in whatever field you practise your profession, you owe it to your clients, your successors and yourselves to make sure your work delivers the outcomes society expects from you; understanding the programme management context in which you operate will help you achieve this.

Sir John Armitt

Acknowledgements

Sponsor:	Dr Edward Wallington, chairman, Programme Management Specific Interest Group (ProgM SIG)
Document manager:	Andrew Kelleher
Second edition authors:	Andrew Gray, Andrew Kelleher, Alan Macklin CBE, Dr Edward Wallington

Thank you to ProgM SIG members, and those from the other specific interest groups (SIGs) who reviewed the early drafts, including: Risk SIG – Kenneth Evans; Enabling Change SIG – Martin Taylor, Simon Williams and Elisabeth Goodman; Portfolio Management SIG – Stephen Parrett; and ProgM SIG – Merv Wyeth.

This second edition is also dedicated to the memory of Paul Rayner, past chairman of ProgM and the APM Programme Management Specific Interest Group, and lead author of the first edition.

Introduction and purpose of guide

The first edition of *APM Introduction to Programme Management* was published over a decade ago and this aspect of the project management profession has come a long way in that short time. The purpose of this guide is to give the reader an insight into programme management – what a programme is, how it functions and how to view it. And who is the reader? Our target audience is those who are relatively new to programme management: an interested stakeholder seeking to engage with a programme about to have a major impact on their life; someone joining a programme team who wants to understand the fundamental principles of programme management; or a member of a project management team seeking to understand how they should interact with a programme – this guide is for you and for anyone like you. This is not a guide for programme management experts – but for anyone less than an expert, this guide should offer you value through its insights or through the opportunities it gives you to compare your first-hand experiences with a 'typical' programme, and thereby gives you the opportunity to challenge what you see going on around you.

Programme management is not about delivering large and complex projects; it is about delivering change – in the physical, professional, business, societal or organisational environment. This publication will help you to understand the organisational and strategic context in which programmes exist, and the differences and relationships between portfolios, programmes, projects and 'business-as-usual' activities, and it highlights some of the keys to understanding successful programme delivery.

APM Introduction to Programme Management 2nd edition is divided into three sections. Section 1 provides an overview of programme management, and Section 2 seeks to explain programme management from the outside looking in through the programme management life cycle. Section 3 aims to offer the reader some conceptual frameworks and insight into what a programme manager should be thinking about in order to optimise the prospects of success and avoid the trap of being drawn into another level of project management.

Programme management – an overview

As programme management practitioners engage with our expanding share of the world, it becomes ever more challenging to satisfy stakeholders while delivering value and benefits in a new and unfamiliar global environment. Programme professionals find themselves operating in complex environments grappling with problems associated with climate change, technological advances, globalisation, sustainable development, overpopulation, security and economic regeneration and growth, as well as bringing about change and transformation in organisational performance. Meeting these challenges requires a systematic approach, implemented in a controlled environment that is founded on sound principles, practices and tools.

Programmes endeavour to deliver change by bringing related projects and activities together in order to manage their relationships, whilst maintaining a strategic view of the work in order to align and coordinate it in support of specific business strategies. Programmes provide a bridge connecting individual projects to a rapidly changing business environment and often a constantly evolving strategy. Programmes are therefore a key delivery mechanism for strategic objectives.

Organisations benefiting most significantly from programme management approaches will normally be those seeking to deliver beneficial and sustainable change to an organisation or society in line with a defined strategy. Where there is change there will be complexity, uncertainty, risk, many interdependencies to manage and conflicting priorities to resolve. By employing sound programme management policy and practices (as opposed to just project management) considerable advantages can be achieved, for example through clearer management focus on the delivery of outcomes and realisation of benefits. Programme management allows the many aspects of the business environment to be abstracted away from the individual component projects, allowing the project manager to focus on delivering the project.

Programme management is still an emerging discipline for delivering transformational change, playing a pivotal role in managing the transition of the solutions developed and delivered by projects into business operations to realise benefits, thus providing the crucial link between strategy and delivery. Where the tools, approaches and mind-sets of practitioners are well developed for project management, those for programme management are still developing: this is an area of opportunity.

1

Programmes and programme management

1.1 What is a programme?

APM Body of Knowledge[1] defines a programme as: "A group of related projects and change management activities that together achieve beneficial change for an organisation."

Programmes are about making lasting change in a controlled manner, so to understand programmes we first need to understand change and change management. *APM Body of Knowledge*[1] states that "change management is a structured approach to moving an organisation from the current state to the desired future state'. This recognises that the conversion of outputs into outcomes and benefits invariably requires some form of business or societal change. Implicit in this is the importance of engaging and influencing the individuals (stakeholders) involved. People will respond to change in various ways, and resistance to change is a natural phenomenon. Managing change in a structured and controlled manner, and in a way that promotes open dialogue with stakeholders is essential if the benefits in a business case are to be realised.

The growing scale of change, the need to respond quickly to changing business environments and the impact of new technologies has led many organisations to adopt programmes as the means of achieving organisational and strategic change. Programmes are temporary management structures designed to help organisations to achieve specific objectives.

The successful delivery of change relies on a systematic approach that manages the relationships, dependencies and interfaces across the organisation. This is integral to the successful delivery of change and the benefits expected to be delivered during the change and onwards once delivered. Change occurs across multiple projects, and may incorporate business-as-usual activities within

[1] *APM Body of Knowledge 6th edition* (2012), available from the Association for Project Management, https://www.apm.org.uk/BOK6

the programme scope, and this needs to be coordinated to ensure success. Thus a programme[2] of change is required, and this needs to be managed to support strategic direction and benefits realisation.

1.1.1 Features of a programme

Programmes may vary in size, type and structure, and how they are applied; however, programmes generally display a similar set of characteristics, as follows:

- Their purpose is to deliver the capability to make strategic, significant or step changes to organisations, or to an organisation's business activities, or to an environment that an organisation is seeking to support – normally referred to as, or measured by, benefits.[3]
- The need for significant improvement will be consistent with the organisation's strategy, and programmes will help to deliver elements of that strategy.
- The realisation of the desired benefits will be achieved only through the coordination and successful completion of a number of component projects and, frequently, their incorporation into business-as-usual.
- Different parts of an organisation or differing organisations may be affected by the programme.
- The overall measure of success will be determined by the actual delivery of the expected benefits, which frequently involves the use of capabilities or facilities created by the programme in an on-going, 'business-as-usual' manner.

APM Body of Knowledge states that "programmes invariably involve significant change. This needs to be coordinated across multiple projects and business-as-usual units". This need to manage and coordinate a programme will be discussed in Section 2.

[2] In some countries the US spelling – program – is normally used, whereas in the United Kingdom this spelling usually refers to software instructions (e.g. a 'computer program').

[3] Sometimes benefits are referred to as outcomes or as business benefits. For brevity, the term 'benefit' will be used throughout this publication. Further guidance on benefits and their management can be found in Section 3.4.

1.1.2 Types of programme

As the mechanisms by which organisations deliver their strategies, programmes are as varied as the organisations that initiate them and the strategies they seek to fulfil. There are many types of programme of change, for example related to information technology (such as rolling out a new technology platform), organisational change (such as during a merger of two organisations or an internal restructure), civil engineering (such as opening a new road) or product development (such as introducing a new mobile phone to the market).

Programmes of change are applied across different industry sectors, including government, telecommunications, finance, transport, energy, manufacturing, defence and utilities, to name a few. As such, programme management as a change delivery mechanism is now in widespread use, although maturity levels in different sectors and different organisational types will vary.

Programmes can also be thought of as business change or transformation programmes, in that they seek to change some aspect of an organisation, or even the organisation itself.

1.1.3 Other interpretations and uses of the term 'programme'

The term 'programme' can mean different things to different people. Programmes come in all shapes and sizes, and the term 'programme' is applied to many different structures. Thus its use and meaning can vary widely across industry sectors and business cultures.

For example, in the construction industry 'programme' often refers to the timetable of activities that must be completed (the schedule), whilst 'programme management' can refer to the process of integrating separate project schedules. As an example, on a large engineering project there may be several contractors, each managing a range of subcontractors – all of whom will produce their own separate schedules of work, referred to as 'programmes' – and the integration of these many schedules into a coherent master schedule would be called 'programme management'.

Also in the construction, utilities and heavy engineering industries the term 'programme management' is often used by contracting organisations to refer to a portfolio of projects that benefit from a consistent or integrated form of management. These projects typically result in deliverables created by a contractor for a client organisation in exchange for payment, and therefore the contractor has a limited interest and influence over the delivery of benefits.

1.2 What is programme management?

APM Body of Knowledge defines programme management as "the coordinated management of projects and change management activities to achieve beneficial change".

Although we focus on the *APM Body of Knowledge* definition in this publication, it is worth noting that other definitions of programme management are available from bodies such as AXELOS (https://www.axelos.com/best-practice-solutions/msp).

Because programmes are the method by which change is delivered in pursuit of strategic objectives, programme management provides a management interface between those responsible for deciding strategy and those responsible for managing the component projects and other activities. Programmes deliver improvement and change that will successfully achieve the desired outcomes, thus establishing the environment for generating benefits aligned to the organisation's objectives within the organisation's cultural and economic environment.

Typical programme management responsibilities include:

- selecting, initiating and monitoring the component projects that make up the programmes, including defining the scope of individual projects;
- progressively developing and re-validating a sound business case;
- managing the expectations of key stakeholders and engaging their support;
- managing risks associated with the internal and external environments;
- coordination between component projects and synchronisation of dependencies;
- managing programme change, such as cancelling projects or changing the scope of projects in reaction to changes in the organisation's strategy or environment;
- coordination of business-as-usual activities where they fall within the defined scope of the programme;
- identifying, supporting, measuring, monitoring and managing the realisation of benefits.

In summary, programme management provides a layer of management, above that of the component project management teams, focused on defining, integrating and coordinating the projects to maximise the value of the combined

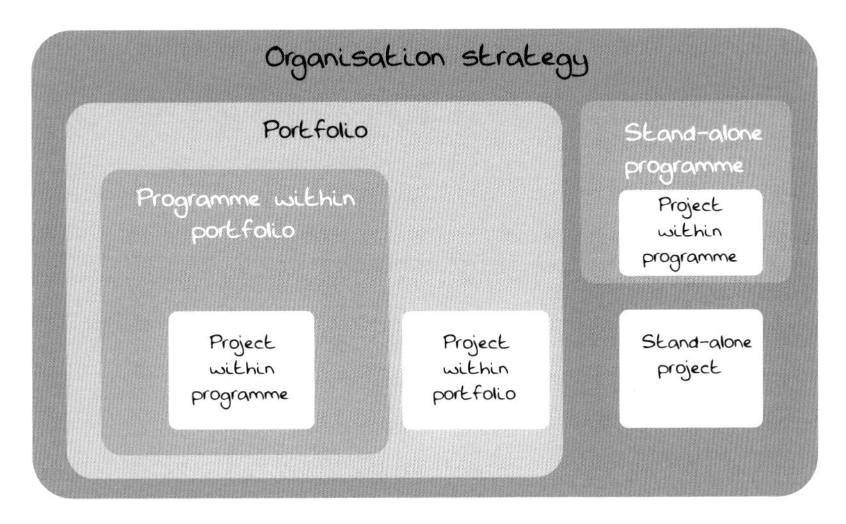

Figure 1.1 Programmes in relation to organisational strategy, portfolios and projects (adapted from *APM Body of Knowledge 6th edition*)

deliverables of the component projects into fully usable capabilities that may be used to deliver the desired benefits and to realise strategic objectives.

For completeness, Figure 1.1 above shows the relationship between programme management, project management and portfolio management. The latter are defined as follows (definitions from *APM Body of Knowledge*):

- Project management is the application of processes, methods, knowledge, skills and experience to achieve the project objectives.
- Portfolio management is the selection, prioritisation and control of an organisation's projects and programmes in line with its strategic objectives and capacity to deliver. The goal is to balance change initiatives and business-as-usual while optimising return on investment.

1.3 Programme management and strategic direction

Strategic planning and setting the direction for an organisation is fundamentally different from operational management. Senior managers and executives deal with uncertainty and ambiguity as they set strategic direction, and then adapt this to address changes and challenges in the environment the organisation is operating in and its direction of travel. Whereas, at a project level, project managers operate with clarity of purpose, for example around cost, timescale and quality targets as defined by the single project.

When project managers work with senior managers these differences in viewpoint and approach can cause friction as the expectations of both parties can be fundamentally different. Programme management teams operate between directors (strategy focus) and project managers (delivery focus). Programme managers' skills are in understanding the strategic direction of the organisation, ensuring that there is an alignment of the suite of projects to support the business objectives, working in an uncertain environment and responding to change with a constant focus on achieving benefits.

When collections of different projects are used to move an organisation towards a strategic change, alongside business-as-usual operations, it is more efficient and beneficial to structure this strategic change as a programme. The benefits of programme delivery are discussed in Section 1.9, and include management and alignment of complex interactions between the outputs of individual projects, outcomes and benefits.

Having a programme management approach allows the organisation's senior managers and directors to focus on setting direction, considering medium and long-term issues, whilst the programme manager will ensure that this is translated into the language of projects, manage the project managers and deliver to the organisation the required changes and capabilities to enable realisation of the desired benefits. In many organisations change programmes tend to cut across business-as-usual structures. For example, a programme transforming a bank's operation to internet-based services will need to interact with the bank's existing vertical and functional structures, i.e. operations, IT, human resources (HR), finance, marketing and so on. The aims and objectives of these groups may not always be aligned and, unless such interactions are carefully planned in conjunction and with the cooperation of each business unit, the programme could run into a 'brick wall' of non-cooperation. Planning and managing such interactions are a key activity within programme management.

Most large organisations can have several change programmes running concurrently. Therefore, the most senior levels of management need to take seriously not only the 'sponsorship' roles for individual programmes, but also the management of the change programmes in a way that recognises the potential multiple points of impact on the stakeholders involved. An organisation's directors must create the environment in which change programmes can succeed in delivering outcomes and benefits, and hence the strategy. Business change and programme management should therefore be well understood by the most senior management in an organisation and be represented at that level.

1.4 How do programmes differ from projects?

While there is frequently overlap between programme and project management activities, it is wrong to regard programmes as merely large and complex projects. They are usually larger than projects, in terms of number of staff and duration, but not necessarily so. Projects generally do not include business-as-usual activities, whereas programmes may include (and certainly interact with) such activities; inclusion of business-as-usual activities and programme composition is generally determined by organisational policy. Programmes have a different purpose and require different management structures and skills to be successful.

Projects are the means to deliver specific one-off deliverables. To be successful, the required deliverables must be defined in advance, with defined budgets and timetable expectations. By contrast, programmes are the means to deliver benefits or outcomes, and amongst their activities are those needed to define and agree the scope of the various projects that will make the achievement of the desired benefits possible. For example, a project might create a new warehouse, i.e. a deliverable. A warehouse on its own may seem to have little direct value, but when it is combined with the deliverables of other projects – such as a computerised stock-control system, a retrained workforce, a new organisational structure, or a new staff bonus scheme – in a programme, it can provide the capability of supplying customers faster, with reduced costs and less wastage due to goods damaged in transit, which are the benefits realised by the programme.

Success for a project is usually defined as creating the required deliverables to an adequate standard, within agreed time and cost constraints. Whether the deliverable, such as a new warehouse, is successfully used or not is not the point. Indeed, there are many projects that have been deemed highly successful, as judged by the project's measures of success, that have created deliverables that have never actually been used. Success for a programme is usually measured in terms of creating a whole new capability and, increasingly, the extent to which the expected benefits are actually realised.

The term programme management is often used to refer to the execution of a number of projects by a contractor, for a client. It could be argued that this is not

Table 1.1 Summary of key differences between programmes and projects

Aspect	Programmes	Projects
Clarity of scope	Programmes involve uncertainty in funding, range and impact.	Projects require clearly defined scope, budget and timescales (agile projects will look to fix scope per iteration).
Clarity of deliverables	Specific deliverables to be created are usually unclear at the start.	The required deliverables are usually clearly defined at the start (agile projects will look to fix deliverables per iteration).
Structure	Separately managed projects, which must be coordinated. The structure may be unclear at the start and may change throughout the life of the programme.	A project forms a single managed entity, which is clear at the start and will not usually change significantly during the life of the project.
Methodologies or approaches	Frequently involves coordinating and managing several different organisations, each of which is responsible for one or more discrete projects, and each of which may be using a different methodology of project approach.	A single project is normally the responsibility of a single organisation, working to a single methodology or project approach.
Clarity of budgets and timescales	At the start, the time and budget required will often be unclear, and part of the role of the programme will be to define these.	Projects start with a project initiation document, project management plan, business case or equivalent that defines expected costs and timescales.
Approach to change	Because the scope and deliverables are unclear, change to priorities and requirements is constant and a major feature of programmes.	Change to scope or desired deliverables are generally subject to rigorous control.
Critical activities	A major element is managing people and organisational issues necessary to ensure that the new capabilities will be used to deliver the desired benefits.	The major element is managing the technology or specialist skills necessary to create the deliverables.
Measure of success	The creation of useable capability and/or the delivery of business benefits.	The creation of the specified deliverables within agreed time and cost constraints.

programme management as we have defined it, and is in fact a series of unrelated projects which happen to share a common set of resources, and likely a common approach and methodology. People have used 'programme' in the past, where we would now use the term 'portfolio of projects'. Examples could include the construction of a number of water treatment plants for a local utility body or a series of retail unit refurbishments by a shop-fitting contractor for a retail chain. If, however, this is a series of related projects, or coordinated delivery of a set of projects that, managed together achieve benefit of a strategic nature, then this is programme management – the key question is 'are they aligned to achieve a combined benefit', or are they just delivering a series of outputs.

However, this work will typically form a part of a larger programme, and it is only at that programme level that benefits will play a key role and be realised. In the case of the water treatment plants, other projects to measure water quality and improve other parts of the infrastructure will combine with the treatment plants to deliver the key performance indicators required by the industry regulator, for example. In the retail example, only when the marketing, management information systems and staff training projects complement the shop refurbishments will the increased income and customer satisfaction benefits become possible.

1.5 How do programmes differ from portfolios?

Portfolio management is the selection, prioritisation and control of an organisation's projects and programmes in line with its strategic objectives and capacity to deliver. The goal is to balance change initiatives and business-as-usual while optimising return on investment[4]. Programme management relates to the coordinated management of a set of related projects – typically where the projects are mutually dependent and all are needed to create the required capability and business benefits – portfolio management is about the capacity of an organisation to manage the totality of its projects and programmes, and the choice of which projects to include in the portfolio to achieve maximum benefit. Portfolio management helps ensure that the right programmes and projects are selected in the first place and regularly reviewed. A portfolio may include all or

[4] For a definition and further guidance on portfolio management, see *APM Body of Knowledge*. Also available at http://knowledge.apm.org.uk/bok/portfolio-management

some programmes and/or projects, and be held at various levels within an organisation or in some parts and not others – there is no one-size-fits-all.

The linking characteristics of a portfolio lie in areas other than benefits. The common factor is usually that all of the projects lie within the same organisation or department, and they must be financed through a common source of funding or they need to make efficient use of a common pool of resources. Thus portfolio management is akin to the similarly named activity that takes place in the financial world, where a portfolio of investments is managed to yield maximum returns and capital growth with acceptable levels of risk. In such a portfolio there is no relationship between the different stocks and shares – each investment is self-contained and is bought or sold only to achieve the objectives of the portfolio as a whole.

Portfolio management helps ensure the efficient use of development resources, such as business analysts, solutions architects, web designers and so on – while minimising costs through the elimination of duplicate management and support activities. It also helps to create an understanding of how the various IT projects will contribute or not to the achievement of strategies of the various business units for which they are being run – something that is not always clear with traditional approaches to project management.

Portfolio management ensures that the portfolio as a whole meets the organisation's objectives, with programmes and projects being added or removed independently of others in the portfolio. Programme management deals with mutually dependent projects, which should only be added to or removed if the result improves the realisation of programme benefits.

Both programme and portfolio management require a similar strategic awareness to be successful, with an overlap of skills, particularly those related to organisational empathy and flexibility. In many cases portfolio management talent comes from the business side of an organisation, whereas a programme manager tends to come from a project background.

1.6 How do we run a programme?

Having a structured approach to how a programme is run is important to successful benefits realisation, as well as to help stakeholders to understand the process they are involved in/affected by. The following 'governance, control and assurance' diagram (Figure 1.2) provides an overview of the programme management environment.

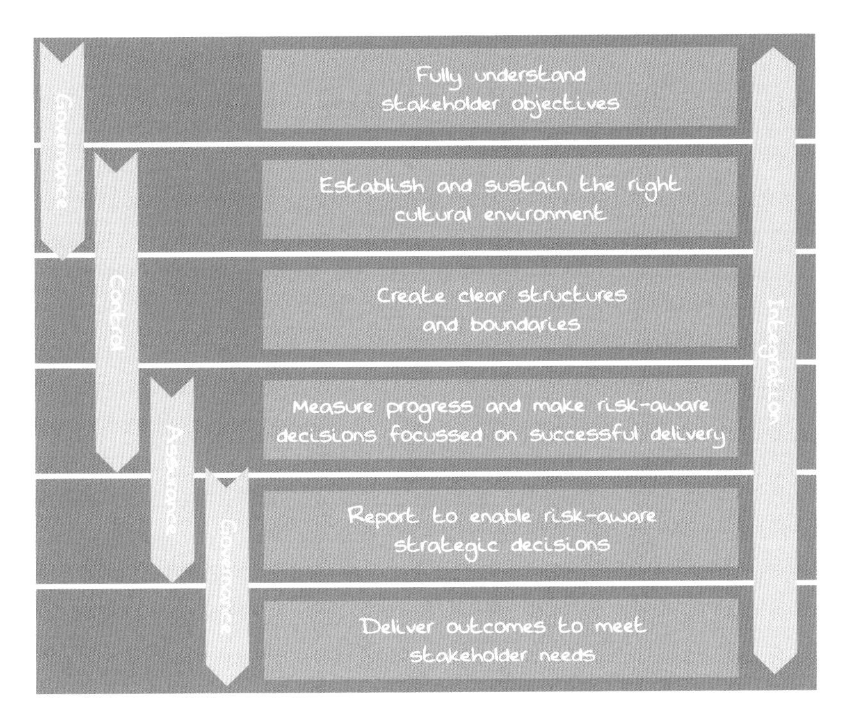

Figure 1.2 Programme governance, control and assurance overview

Adapted from *Driving the successful delivery of major defence projects: Effective control is a key factor in successful projects*, National Audit Office, HC 30 Session 2005–2006, 20 May 2005. Provided courtesy of BMT Hi-Q Sigma Ltd.

There are a number of activities undertaken during a programme, as shown in Figure 1.2 in the central rectangular boxes. The day-to-day management of a programme comes down to four main principles – governance, control, assurance and integration. The first principle of governance looks to ensure that we understand stakeholder objectives and business requirements (i.e. what do we want to achieve) and to establish the programme environment foundations. Stakeholder objectives and business requirements can change over the life cycle of the programme, so these need to be constantly engaged, considered and adjusted and impacts communicated; stakeholder engagement is a continuous requirement, and feeds into the change management strategy. Control is then used to make sure the environment is maintained and adapted as required, that all are clear on the structure and working boundaries (both for the programme as a whole and for its constituent parts), and that progress is made and measured. Assurance provides a process to maintain and monitor progress and to support risk-based decision making focused on successful delivery. A final layer of governance enables risk-based strategic decision making on the programme (and feeding into organisational strategy), and ensures a focus on delivery of outcomes to meet stakeholder needs. These principles should not be seen as mutually exclusive, and that integration across the programme is a key principle in its own right.

Many organisations look to standard models when trying to improve their project and programme management practice. A number of these are discussed in the APM publication *Models to Improve the Management of Projects*.[5]

We explore the running of a programme and the programme life cycle in Section 2. In Section 3 we explore programme assessment by means of conceptual frameworks that focus on supporting elements to allow a programme to be successful. These frameworks highlight areas for consideration when running a programme, and help define organisational capability to run a successful programme. We explore a number of frameworks and then assess lenses of use as defined in P3M3®[6], which is a maturity model and provides a framework that

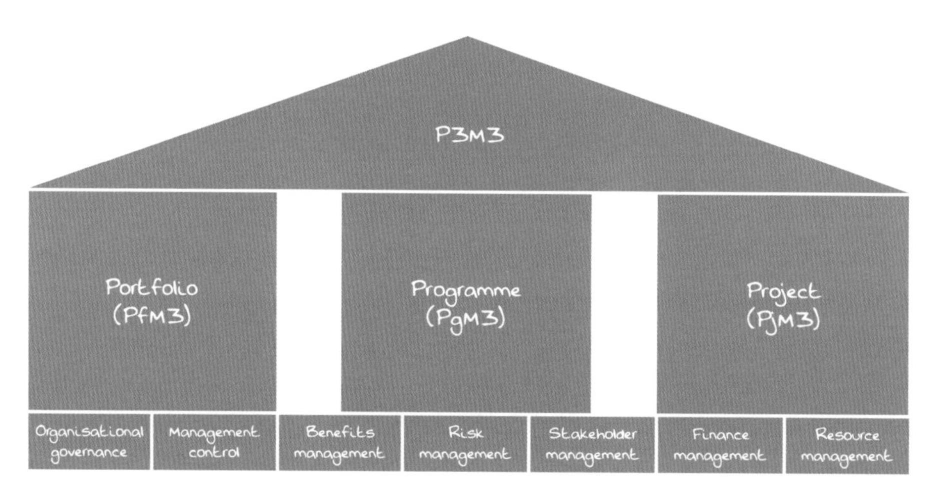

Figure 1.3 P3M3® framework

5 APM *Models to Improve the Management of Projects*, available at – https://www.apm.org.uk/M2IMP

6 Portfolio, Programme and Project Management Maturity Model (P3M3); see https://www.axelos.com/best-practice-solutions/p3m3/what-is-p3m3 for further details. P3M3® is a registered trade mark of AXELOS Limited. All rights reserved.

organisations can use to assess their current performance and plan for improvement when managing and delivering change.

Each sub-model is further broken down into seven Perspectives (explored in greater detail in Section 3), each of which are important to success:

- Organisational governance.
- Management control.
- Benefits management.
- Risk management.
- Stakeholder management.
- Finance management.
- Resource management.

1.7 Who runs a programme?

The successful delivery of a programme of change is largely dependent on the range of people involved in the programme, and links to the governance, control, integration and assurance principles discussed in Section 1.6. Business change and programme management should be well understood by the senior management in an organisation, and be represented at that level, as the impact of programmes on strategic objectives is crucial to business success. The role of senior managers includes setting the culture, environment and motivation that underpins programme success. Table 1.2 provides a summary of key roles and responsibilities in a programme, and we expand on some of these below. Further details can be found in *APM Body of Knowledge* and *APM Competence Framework*.

The programme sponsor – also known as the senior responsible owner (SRO) – selected from the senior executive team of the organisation, is ultimately accountable for the programme, and this role should not be delegated. The sponsor owns the vision and business case for the programme, and is responsible for providing direction and leadership for the delivery and implementation of the programme, as well as being accountable for outcomes.

The programme is led by the sponsor, who chairs the programme board, provides governance and leadership to the programme, as well as assessing external factors that may influence the programme, e.g. a change in strategy or external pressures from other programmes or activities, which may impact the programme. The programme board includes the programme manager,

Table 1.2 Roles and responsibilities in a programme

Role	Responsibility
Programme sponsor or senior responsible owner	Fully empowered leadership of individual programmes; owns business case and vision.
Programme manager	Responsible for delivering new capabilities.
Business change manager	Responsible for realising benefits through embedding the change into business-as-usual. Responsible for ensuring their own business area is ready to use the programme's project outputs.
Project manager	Responsible for delivery of project outputs within agreed constraints.
Senior suppliers	Represents the interests of parties involved from supplier perspective (internal or external).
Senior users	Responsible for ensuring the needs of those that will use outputs are met.
Communications manager	Responsible for the identification, analysis, planning and implementation of programme communications.
Stakeholder manager	Responsible for the identification, analysis, planning and implementation of actions designed to engage with stakeholders.
Risk and issues manager	Establishes, facilitates and maintains the threat, opportunity and issues management cycle.
Programme management office (PMO)	Support body for key roles, providing advice, challenge and checks.

representatives from the customer and supplier (both of which could be internal or external customers or suppliers), business change manager(s) (who will oversee transition of the change) and others as appropriate.

The programme manager reports to the programme board on a regular basis. The programme manager is primarily focused on managing relations, dependencies and integration between the programme's constituent parts. The programme manager is typically backed by a programme management office[7] (PMO), which will support the effective running of the programme (which could include training, communications, resource management and allocation, monitoring performance

[7] For further information on the role of the programme management office and the programme infrastructure, refer to *APM Body of Knowledge 6th edition*, Chapter 1.1.4, 'Infrastructure'.

and progress, reporting etc.). Further details on PMOs can be sought from the APM Project Management Office Specific Interest Group[8].

Reporting to the programme manager will be a series of project managers who will control their individual projects as part of the programme. The programme should also be acutely aware of stakeholders associated with it, and many programmes may include a stakeholder manager. A communications manager often appears in programmes, and will be responsible for creating and managing a communication plan to ensure all parties (often including the public) are kept aware and up to date with programme objectives and progress.

For further detail in this area, refer to the *APM Competence Framework*[9] and *APM Body of Knowledge*.

1.8 How programmes deliver benefits

The *APM Body of Knowledge* states that benefits associated with strategic organisational change are delivered through programmes of multiple-aligned projects and change management activity. Such programmes can contain complex interactions between the outputs of individual projects, outcomes and benefits.

The role of the programme is to deliver outcomes, and hence set the scene for delivering benefits, as opposed to the outputs that an individual project delivers. Gaining shared stakeholder clarity, understanding and commitment to the desired outcomes is critical to programme success. Wherever possible, the programme should seek to realise measurable benefits early and then frequently during its life. However, it is likely that most benefits will be realised during business-as-usual use of the programme outcomes (e.g. a new facility, new structure or new capabilities), and likely once the programme ends. Where benefits are realised after the programme team has been disbanded or assigned to new endeavours, responsibility for monitoring, measuring and realising the benefits must be transferred to an appropriate function. The transition plan should be considered as part of programme planning, and discussed and agreed with the programme board and business change manager.

A critical component within benefit management is the project(s) or set of activities needed to manage the transition from the old ways of working, based on previous processes, tools and capabilities, to the new ways. Such transitions

[8] *APM PMO SIG*: see – https://www.apm.org.uk/group/apm-pmo-specific-interest-group

[9] *APM Competence Framework*: see – https://www.apm.org.uk/competenceframework

are frequently very complex and risky. For example, they may involve the switch-off of old systems or facilities and the switch-on of new ones according to tight timescales. They depend upon the commitment of users and line management who are not directly under the control of the programme or any of its component projects. Furthermore, there can be little allowance for failure or delay, since service to customers must continue throughout the transition and, unless a smooth transition is effected, it may not be possible for the organisation to take advantage of the new capabilities and thus be able to realise the benefits that the programme is intended to provide.

It is important to implement a consistent approach to benefits management across a programme, particularly for consistency of measurement. Without a consistent approach, it is difficult to aggregate benefits across multiple projects and to assess their collective impact on business performance across the organisation. Benefits management ensures the realisation of benefits, and responsibility for it may rest partly with the programme management team and partly with another group, such as the main board or the organisation's finance function. We discuss benefits management further in Section 3.4.

The relationship between projects, programmes and benefit delivery is outlined in Figure 1.4, which shows how the deliverables created by projects are combined by programmes to create capabilities, which are then used to realise benefits.

1.9 What challenges are faced?

As with any change, and related change management activity, programme management can face a number of intrinsic challenges. These are all surmountable, especially when considered continuously during the programme life cycle, and through lessons learned from other programmes.

Typical challenges experienced include:

- managing the complexity and natural tension that exists between corporate strategies, the delivery mechanisms (i.e. projects) and the business-as-usual environments – this level of complexity can easily be underestimated;
- gaining corporate board level support to provide leadership, commitment and sponsorship;
- application of adequate strength of leadership from the programme board, programme manager and supporting structures;

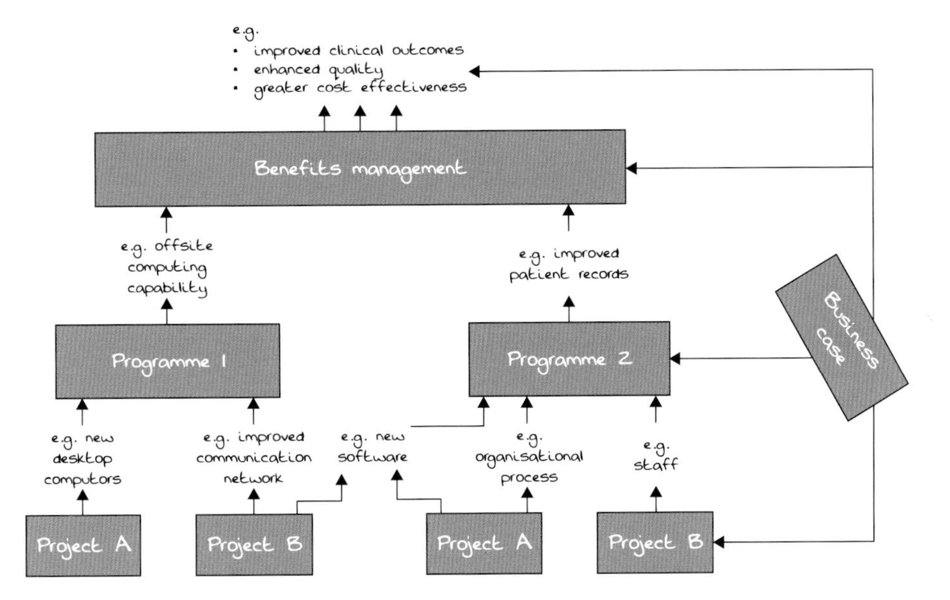

Figure 1.4 The relationship between projects, programmes and benefits

- defining and maintaining a clear vision and a real picture (blueprint) of the future capability required, as well as metrics to monitor progress towards the vision;
- maintaining an adequate focus on benefits, which needs to be built in from the start and monitored throughout; as well as looking to realise benefits as early as possible;
- addressing the tensions that arise between programme targets and constraints (for example across scope, cost, time, risk, benefits etc.);
- transitioning the desired/necessary cultural changes – the people/human element can often be overlooked;
- gaining the required levels of stakeholder engagement – this is particularly important as the programme will likely deliver significant change, and this needs to be understood and agreed;
- managing programme interdependencies;
- ensuring a clear requirements capture and management approach across the programme.

The following sections provide an overview of 'the programme life cycle' and 'programme assessment', which when applied, support the programme progression and help mitigate the above challenges.

2

The programme life cycle

2.1 A high level programme management life cycle

In spite of the variation in size of programmes, from a handful of people and a few projects through to thousands of people on large, complex undertakings, each one can be deemed to follow a standard life cycle. The key phases of this standard programme life cycle are shown in Figure 2.1.

Other representations of programme life cycles may vary in terminology for the individual phases, but each follows the fundamental principles of concept, definition, delivery and closure. It should also be noted that some representations (or organisations) might use additional sub-phases to those proposed here.

It is important in life cycle terms to differentiate between the steady-state operations of a business (or of a social environment) and the change itself. Figure 2.2 illustrates how a programme is aimed at introducing change, not at running the steady-state activities, and how these different elements align with

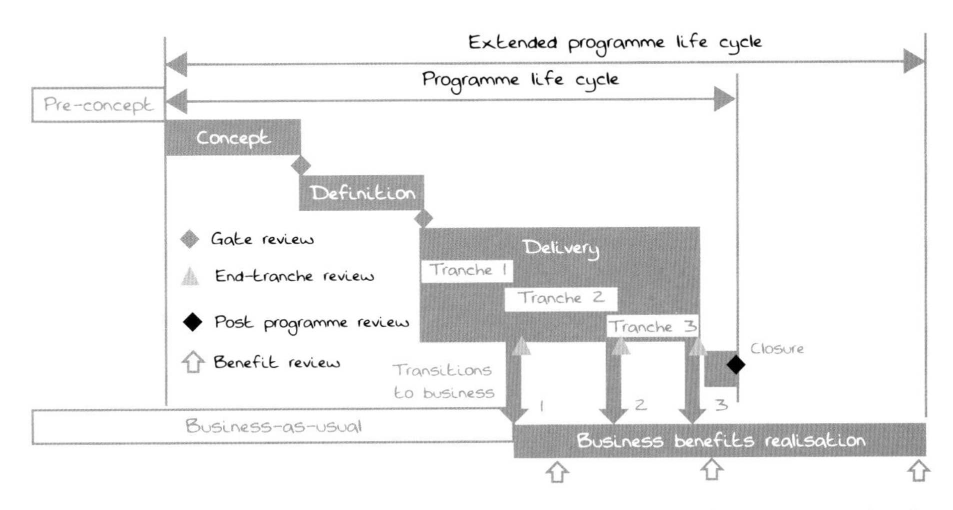

Figure 2.1 Programme life cycle representation (adapted from *APM Body of Knowledge*, Chapter 1.1.6).

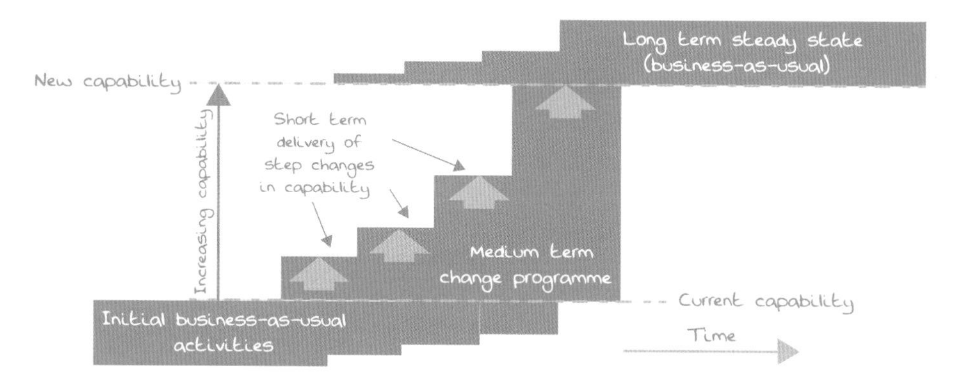

Figure 2.2 Change programme vs. steady-state activities

perceptions of short, medium and long-term timescales. Programmes typically develop change by stepping through sub-divisions that facilitate approval gates and deliver increments in capability (these are known as tranches[10]) with resulting transitions into the business operations (or social environment), as illustrated in Figures 2.1 and 2.2.

The programme life cycle is aimed at establishing a firm platform for the overall change journey, whether this is for a business or societal transformation, the introduction of a new capability, or the launch of a new product into its operating environment. Figure 2.3 shows one conceptual description of this journey, illustrating the key relationships between the business objectives, the definition of the programme, the individual projects and their outputs, the programme outputs and the resulting benefits, and how these underpin the resulting business performance.

2.2 Life cycle strategy considerations

Prior to the start of a programme, there may be a period of uncertainty while an organisation understands and decides that a change of some description is required and that some form of investment in change is needed. In some cases this may be a formally recognised strategic phase of activities (for example, it may be called a 'genesis', 'foundation' or 'pre-concept' phase), and in others it may be less clearly

[10] Tranches are covered in greater detail in Section 2.5.

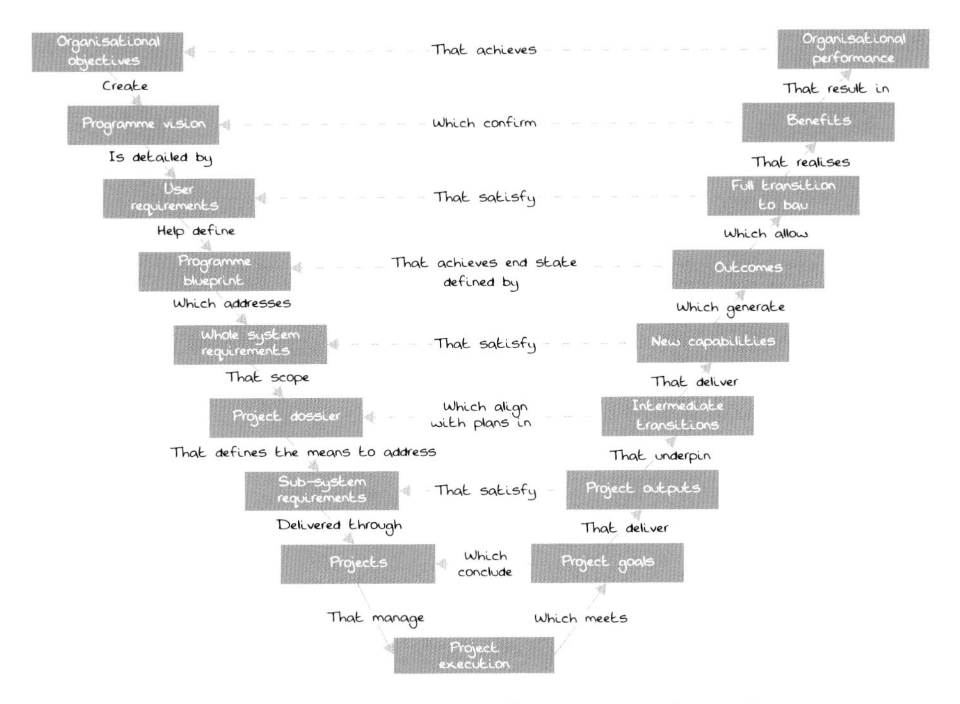

Figure 2.3 Conceptual representation of programme change journey showing validation and verification relationships based on the Vee Model

defined or revolutionary. In theory, all organisations should have clearly defined and agreed business change strategies, the implementation of which requires the initiation of programmes. Indeed, if the organisation is undertaking programmes within the framework of portfolio management then the programmes will be fully aligned with strategic plans.[11] Within such an environment (or where the business undertakes regular change or introduction of new complex products), the business will have defined a business change life cycle specific to its needs, and so the individual programme life cycle will have to be aligned with this generic business framework. This alignment is an important part of defining a specific strategy for the overall programme approaches, i.e. the definition of its programme life cycle.

Another important consideration for the programme life cycle is the selection of the *approach* the organisation would like to take in the delivery phase of an individual programme (or potentially introducing the overall change through

[11] For further information, refer to *APM Body of Knowledge 6th edition*, Chapter 1.1.3, 'Portfolio management'.

related programmes). Different forms of programme approaches are described in Table 2.1.

The definitions in Table 2.1 are also applicable to different programme phases, or to individual tranches within the delivery phase. Depending on the level of uncertainty during the concept or definition phases, it may be necessary to conduct 'discovery' or 'pilot' projects, undertake feasibility studies or to create proof-of-concept systems in order to help clarify the programme life cycle strategy.

Therefore, the idealised programme life cycle shown in Figure 2.4 should be adapted to suit the nature of the change and the environment in which the change is to be undertaken.

Table 2.1 Different programme life cycle strategic approaches

Approach	Description
Linear	Where the business transitions to the final new state through a single sequential series of activities each providing only partial capability (possibly even in a single tranche). This is suitable for stable, low-risk environments where the full benefit can be delivered through a single final roll-out.[12]
Incremental	Where the transition to the new state is achieved through a staged series of smaller step changes in capability delivering increasing benefit. This is an approach that can deliver 'quick wins' to help engage stakeholders in an uncertain environment and build confidence towards the final end state, and is well represented within the 'tranche' framework.
Experimental	Where the programme runs parallel activities in order to explore high-risk options and fall-backs, where the way forward is unclear at first. The scope of this type of activity will depend on the risk appetite of the organisation – in some circumstances the approach may extend for the duration of the delivery phase.
Evolutionary	In this approach the programme takes a number of planned full transitions to business-as-usual, each of which are based on user/customer feedback from the preceding transition and implementation. This approach can be used for time-critical initial entry to market followed by follow-on solutions, but runs a possible risk of negative reputational impacts from continuous changes.

[12] The term 'big bang' is often used in these situations. Depending on the circumstances there may be considerable overlap between this definition and that of an 'extended project', which encompasses transition to operations and realisation of benefits.

There are many permutations, combinations and overlaps in life cycle strategy definition: the critical elements are to define the way forward such that it can be clearly communicated to the team, the sponsor and to the other stakeholders, and underpin the overall programme detailed definition. This is a key programme decision as it can have major implications downstream on the management style and behaviours.

The programme life cycle strategy should also incorporate or reflect any issues arising from an appreciation of the likely development methodologies used at the project level. These may be driven by the nature of the work in those projects and the level of threats to successful project conclusions. They also need to be integrated into the wider programme environment.

An example of this would be programmes undertaken within an agile development environment and/or where one or more projects employ agile development techniques.[13] It should be noted that an appropriate, robust and tailored programme management environment is entirely conducive and applicable to an agile development environment.[14]

Finally, consideration must also be given to the nature and strengths of the tensions that will be prevalent within the programme environment, and how the overall programme approach may be adapted to reflect or respond to these. Figure 2.4 illustrates some of these tensions.

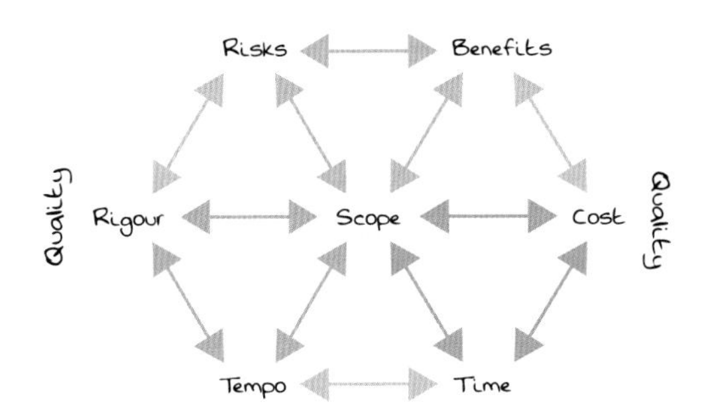

Figure 2.4 Typical programme tensions to be addressed[15]

[13] Note that employing agile development techniques in a business environment that is not suited to them restricts the probability of overall success. For a discussion of when to select agile/non-agile project approaches, refer to *The Practical Adoption of Agile Methodologies*, 2015, Princes Risborough: APM.

[14] For example the AgilePgM™ framework, available from the DSDM Consortium (www.dsdm.org).

[15] Taken from *Valuing Our Place in the World – Using Systems Engineering in Programme and Project Management*, Gray, A. and Richardson, K., INCOSE UK Annual Systems Engineering Conference 2015.

2.3 Programme life cycle governance

The programme life cycle provides a framework to support the principles of good organisational and programme governance.[16] One of these principles is that the programme approach should have authorisation points at which the business case, inclusive of strategy alignment, cost, benefit and risk, is reviewed. These authorisation points can take the form of gateway reviews between phases, and individual stage or gate reviews within the phases, as shown in Figure 2.1.

The exact nature of these reviews depends on the organisation, but they should ensure that positive business decisions are taken to continue with the programme in its current direction, change direction or abandon the programme completely. The reviews also provide ideal opportunities to ensure that all governance principles are being followed.

Programme gate reviews should also occur at the end of each tranche in the delivery phase, to formally authorise moving to the next tranche, assess programme performance and any benefit realisation to that point. These will also be aligned with, and cascade up from, stage gate reviews in the individual projects.

2.4 Programme concept[17] phase

2.4.1 Purpose

The purpose of this phase is to identify a programme, its vision, aims and strategic alignment such that clear foundations are set for successive activities and communicated to programme team members and external stakeholders. This culminates in the outline business case.

2.4.2 Overview

An overview of the concept phase activities, inputs, outputs, controls and supporting mechanisms is given in Figure 2.5.

[16] Refer also to *Directing Change: A Guide to the Governance of Project Management*, 2011, Princes Risborough: APM.

[17] This document uses the phase labels as defined in the *APM Body of Knowledge 6th edition*. This phase is also known elsewhere as the 'identification' phase.

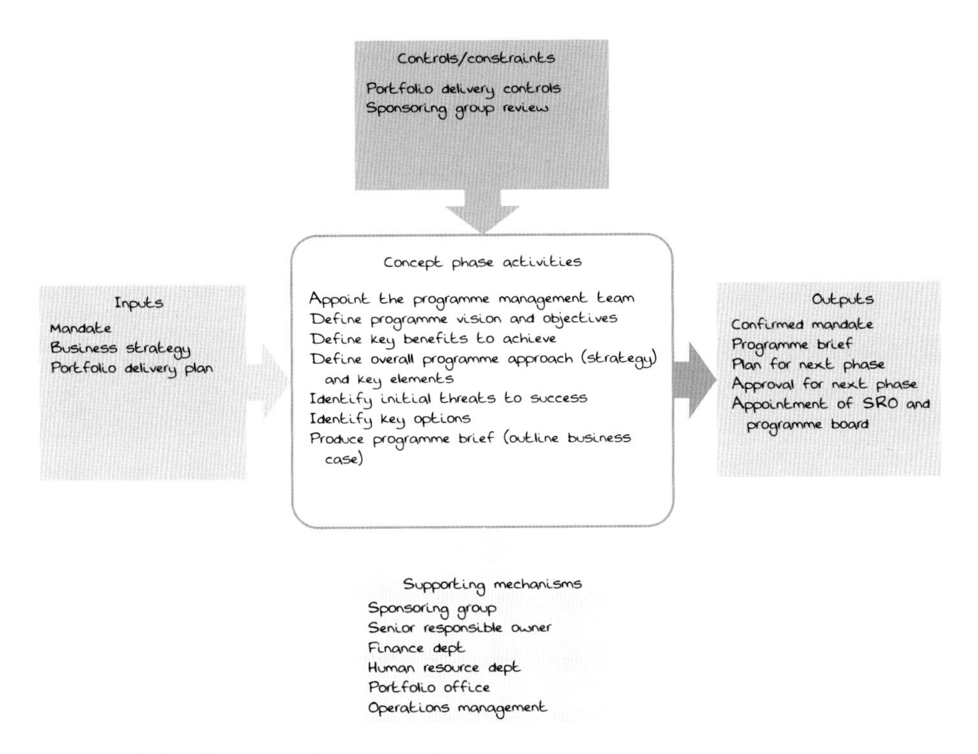

Figure 2.5 Concept phase overview

2.4.3 Key activities

This phase can be initiated on receipt of an initial mandate (or similar form of instruction from a sponsoring group) or, where no such mandate formally exists, the start of the phase can be a gradual 'morphing' from other business activities as the initial mandate is defined. This mandate can take the form of a simple written instruction or a strategic business case that outlines the desires of the organisation in terms of outcomes expected against strategic business objectives. Depending on the business environment, it can be generated through organisational business policies and planning, an overarching portfolio strategy and plan, or a preceding 'pre-concept' phase.

The main aims of this phase are to confirm the programme vision and mandate, define the programme organisational arrangements, produce the programme brief and achieve a decision on the outline business case. The programme brief describes the basic validity and viability of the programme. It will encapsulate the vision, objectives and benefits to be achieved, and estimated cost and timescales in order to achieve those benefits. Risks to achieving the objectives will be outlined, as well as various options and opportunities that have been identified.

The programme organisations to be defined include the governance structure (i.e. the arrangement of the sponsor and the programme board) and the composition of the programme management office (PMO). The PMO may be a stand-alone support office, or it may be integrated within a wider portfolio management office.

The brief, the programme arrangements and a plan for the Programme definition phase will be reviewed by the business senior management team (which could be an executive board, an investment committee or a portfolio direction group) and, if approved, the programme will then progress to the definition phase. Note that the senior management team may also be known as a 'sponsoring group' (as shown in Figure 2.5).

2.4.4 Relevant *Body of Knowledge* sections

The following sections of *APM Body of Knowledge* provide further information on this phase (other sections of *APM Body of Knowledge* can also provide information):

1.1.5 Knowledge management
1.1.6 Life cycle
1.1.8 Sponsorship
1.2.1 Environment
1.2.3 Strategic management
2.1.5 Leadership

2.5 Programme definition[18] phase

2.5.1 Purpose

The purpose of the definition phase is to establish and gain approval for the programme to proceed, and define it in such a manner that it will be possible to coordinate its component activities and therefore deliver its objectives effectively.

2.5.2 Overview

An overview of the definition phase activities, inputs, outputs, controls and supporting mechanisms is given in Figure 2.6.

[18] Also known as an 'initiation' phase.

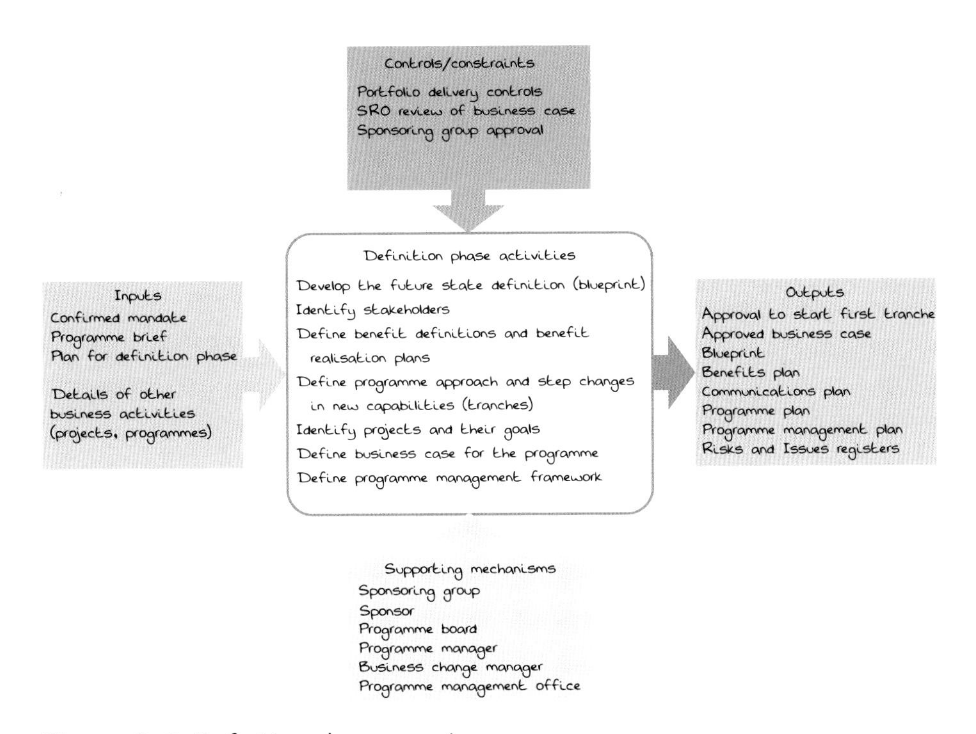

Figure 2.6 Definition phase overview

2.5.3 Key activities

The main thrust of this phase is to achieve a robust definition of the programme such that approval can be sought by the sponsor from the business senior management team/sponsoring group for the programme to proceed. This is achieved by generating a business case defining the objectives, expected benefits, investment required, costs, timescales, risks and ability to achieve the desired objectives. A good breakdown of the typical contents of a business case is provided by the 'Green Book' from HMT[19], which describes a '5 Case Model' where the business case comprises:

- a **strategic** case – the rationale for why you need to undertake the programme;
- an **economic** case – the cost/benefit analysis of the available options;
- a **commercial** case – the viability of any procurement approach;

[19] In particular, refer to *Public Sector Business Cases Using the 5 Case Model* (HM Treasury Green Book supplementary guidance), available from https://www.gov.uk/government/publications/the-green-book-appraisal-and-evaluation-in-central-governent [sic].

- a **financial** case – the affordability of the overall programme;
- a **management** case – the achievability of the programme (in terms of its execution).

The business case therefore requires inputs such as a definition or depiction of the aspects of the future state of the business that is able to meet the objectives of the mandate. This definition (often referred to as the programme blueprint) provides a foundation for the subsequent planning and a focus for the programme as a whole. The future state is defined in terms of future capabilities, organisational structures, personnel (including skills and expertise requirements), processes and workflows, physical infrastructure and technology, and information needed to run the business.

A key element of the business case, and the programme to follow, is the identification and analysis of the benefits that are expected, and what activities, outcomes and specific outputs are needed to realise these benefits. Analysis of the required benefits, the impact on stakeholders and how best to engage and support them and the step changes in business capability needed to achieve the benefits, will help define the delivery of the overall programme. These step changes are known as tranches, and these are aimed towards delivering intermediate capabilities and ultimately the realisation of benefits, as illustrated in Figure 2.7.

Analysis of the programme delivery requirements will help define the projects that are needed to deliver the necessary outputs. Projects can exist within

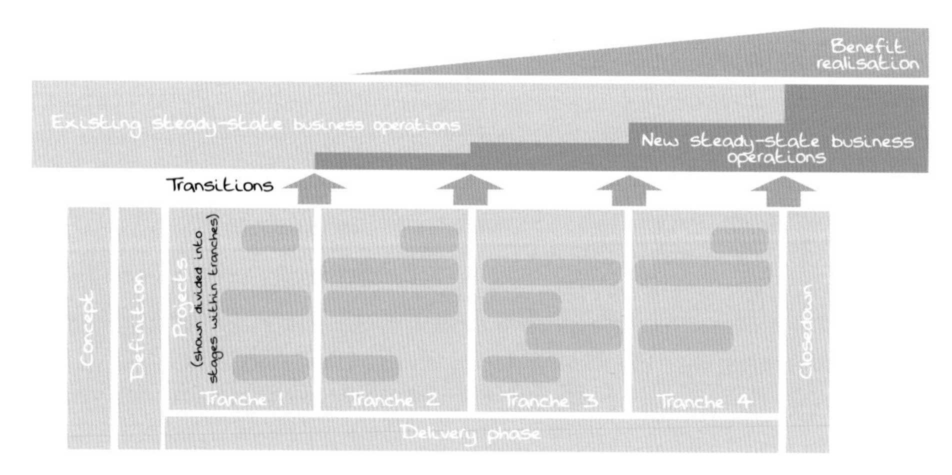

Figure 2.7 Tranches and projects within the delivery phase. (Number of tranches and projects is for illustration only)

tranches, or can span tranches (in which case they will typically be broken into project stages that align with the tranches). Each identified project is then defined individually and makes up an overall dossier of projects within the programme.

In addition, the programme team will undertake identification and analysis of the stakeholders involved in the programme, and then devise a communication and engagement plan to help interact with these stakeholders. Management of stakeholder engagement is critical to the success of a programme, and a key part of the future activities of the central programme team.

The blueprint generation, risk analysis, benefits definition and stakeholder analysis is all carried out in parallel (in an iterative manner) to arrive at the business case. During the phase the programme governance arrangements are also defined and these, along with the overall management framework and the information defined in the blueprint and business case, are used to generate the programme management plan (also known as the programme definition document).

2.5.4 Relevant *Body of Knowledge* sections

The following sections of *APM Body of Knowledge* provide further information on the elements of the definition phase (other sections of *APM Body of Knowledge* also provide information):

1.1.5 Knowledge management	3.1.5 Planning	3.2.6 Solutions development
2.1.1 Communication	3.1.6 Stakeholder management	3.3.1 Resource scheduling
2.1.3 Delegation	3.2.1 Benefits management	3.3.2 Time scheduling
3.1.1 Business case	3.2.4 Change management	3.4.2 Funding
3.1.4 Organisation	3.2.5 Requirement management	3.4.3 Investment appraisal

2.6 Programme delivery[20] phase

2.6.1 Purpose

The purpose of the delivery phase is to manage the programme to deliver what has been planned – including any organisational change and business benefits – in accordance with agreed cost, benefit, time and resource constraints.

[20] Also known as the 'execution' phase.

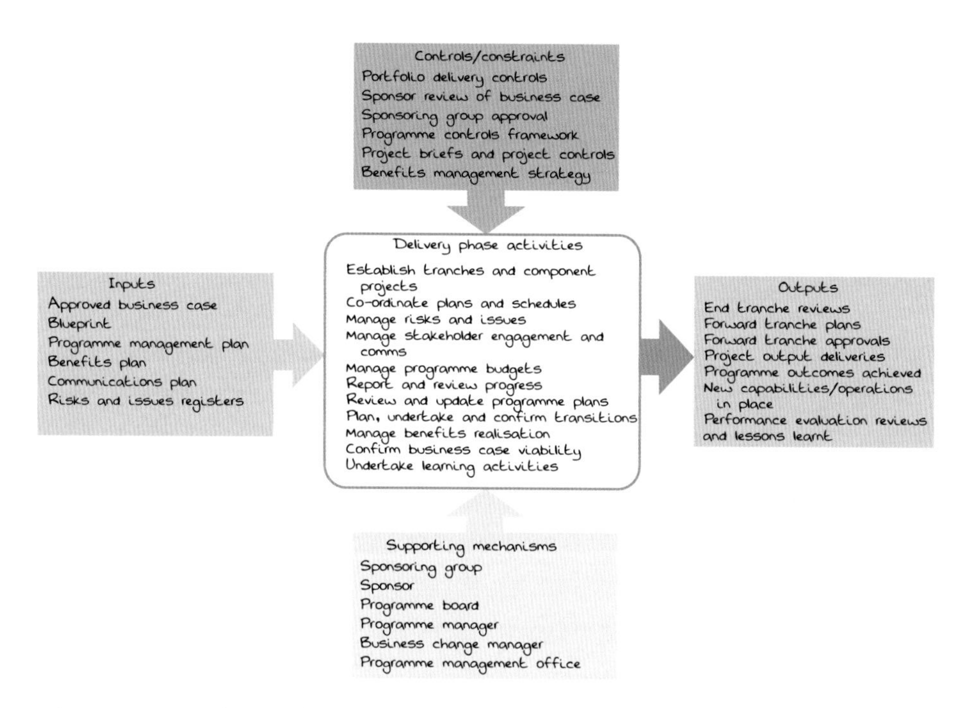

Figure 2.8 Delivery phase overview

2.6.2 Overview

An overview of the delivery phase activities, inputs, outputs, controls and supporting mechanisms is given in Figure 2.8.

2.6.3 Key activities

Once the programme is established, the component projects are created to produce their required outputs according to the programme management plan. These outputs will then be combined under the control of the programme to produce the new capabilities/outcomes that can then be exploited to realise the benefits to the organisation and other stakeholders.

These outcomes cannot be implemented without a transition from the programme to the normal working practices, and this transition is a critical part of the programme management activity. This activity is also the foundation of benefits realisation, where the programme works with the day-to-day business environment to ensure that the business case for the programme is being achieved.

The following sub-sections explore more closely the activities shown in Figure 2.7 grouped under programme delivery, transition and benefits realisation.

i. Programme delivery

Establish tranches and component projects

The component projects themselves must be established and planned in detail, cross-checked and optimised for technical, managerial and commercial consistency. The individual project plans, time schedules and other supporting documentation should be reviewed (by the programme manager or the PMO on their behalf) to ensure consistency and to identify dependencies and potential conflicts.

Ideally for each project a separate project manager should be appointed, although circumstances (such as small-scale projects or projects not overlapping) may allow an individual to run separate projects. Managing a project that is part of a larger programme is different from managing a stand-alone project (for example dealing with decisions made for the greater benefit of the wider programme but penalising for the individual project), and appropriate terms of reference, identifying different reporting structures and escalation procedures, should be provided, agreed and signed off. This is done by expanding the information on each project into separate project briefs (or project initiation documents) and placing project-specific information into these documents (common information is held in the programme management plan/programme definition document).

Detailed project plans will be devised only for the tranche to be executed – activities within future tranches will be defined as the active tranche draws to a close – but the programme definition document will describe the outline timescales and intentions for future tranches. Therefore project briefs are updated at the beginning of each tranche.

Coordinate plans and schedules

Although each component project will develop its own project plan and attendant time schedule, successful programme management requires these to be coordinated, and on a rolling basis. This requires all interdependencies to be identified, and then the individual plans and schedules adjusted to achieve the best possible overall compromise.

Once a consolidated schedule has been agreed, with interdependencies confirmed, it is likely to need constant adjustment as progress and changes are notified to ensure that any delay in one component project is accommodated, thus avoiding 'knock on' delays to other projects and thus to the delivery of the desired programme outcomes.

Through the coordinated management of the component projects, the programme will deliver the required outputs and outcomes in the most cost-efficient manner. Project interface and interdependency management is a key function of the programme environment, for dependencies within the programme and across the programme boundary (inputs from outside the programme).

Manage risks[21]

As with individual projects, rigorous threat, issue and opportunity management is essential. Typically, each project will maintain its own risk register and manage its own risks, but will escalate to a programme-level risk register those risks that are beyond its control, or would have a detrimental impact on another project, or which could be more effectively managed at the programme level.[22] The programme risk register also holds risks for projects that are not yet underway, threats to project interdependencies and programme coordination, or those threats arising from the environment outside the programme (see Section 3.5). The programme team will monitor external situations on behalf of the projects ('boundary scanning') and escalate risks beyond the control or scope of the programme to strategic business or portfolio management.

Manage stakeholder engagement and communications

While coordinating and managing the component projects within the programme, the programme team must also develop relationships with the customer, users, beneficiaries and other stakeholders, undertake consolidated analysis and coordinate the engagement and communications with stakeholders across the projects. Individual projects may undertake their own stakeholder management, but it must be consistent and aligned with the overall programme activity.

[21] Note that the term 'risk' in this section embraces threat, opportunity and issue management.

[22] For example, risks where the responses (actions) are dispersed across many projects.

In complex environments, such as those relating to programmes, stakeholder engagement should be an integral component of all management activities. It must be part of the overall approach to gaining and then maintaining the support and cooperation of all stakeholders, and must be coordinated with related activities such as: governing the programme; communicating risks and progress; and collaborative problem solving.

Manage programme resources and budgets[23]

The programme will monitor and control expenditures against the budgets laid out in the business case and detailed in the programme plan. Overall programme budgets – in terms of total forecast costs and timescales – will have a degree of uncertainty according to the programme maturity and nature of the programme, but each current tranche should have targets set as part of the tranche planning process. The programme manager should have a programme budget composed of:

- funds allocated to on-going projects;
- funds reserved for future planned projects;
- funds allocated to programme-level activities (such as the PMO);
- funding held for programme-level risks, and any risk reserve held on behalf of the projects;
- contingency held for unforeseen events (which will typically reflect the level of programme uncertainty).

The contingency and management reserve held at the programme level may be held on behalf of the individual projects (as well as the programme activities), or an amount may be allocated to the projects to be managed accordingly within the project (with the total across all projects plus the remaining reserve held by the programme equal to the overall programme exposure). This depends on how the various risks are to be owned and managed, and how the individual projects are run. In either case it is important to clarify what contingencies and reserves are being held at which level and for what purpose, to avoid double accounting or gaps.

[23] In this context, the term 'budget' covers not only financial allocations, but also timescales and any other parameter that has a form of intended consumption.

Budgetary control may be exercised through the setting of tolerances on time, costs etc., where individual projects will only have to notify the programme of any intended expenditure outside the permitted variation.

The setting of budgets for tranches, and the increasing maturity of forward estimates from tranche to tranche, can be aligned with business financial approval cycles and processes by adjusting the timings of the tranches themselves.

Report and review progress

At agreed intervals, consolidated programme status reports should be produced. The scope and coverage of these will have been defined during the programme initiation phase according to the needs of the programme board.

Typically such reporting will include programme and financial status reports – based upon information provided by the component projects. These should be a concise 'snapshot' of the status of the programme, identifying progress against milestones and any major new risks, and concentrating on exceptions and departures from agreed plans. A key part of such a report will be progress made towards the delivery of benefits. The financial status report should give a summary of the consolidated costs, revenues, working capital and reserves of the programme.

Producing these reports will require each project to prepare its own individual reports and then forward these to the programme for consolidation and review, normally by the PMO. To ensure that meaningful results can be prepared by the agreed dates, it will normally be necessary for the PMO to define and enforce a standard reporting timetable and to provide templates in which the managers of component projects can record their information. However, the programme must be cognisant of, and respect, the different project environments as individual project reporting will be influenced by the nature of the projects themselves – some projects may be operating in an agile development environment – but it is the role of the programme to consolidate them in a manner appropriate to the needs of the organisation.

In conjunction with the reporting requirements, it is good practice for the programme board to conduct progress reviews at critical points in the life of the programme, such as the end of a design or development phase or immediately before beginning implementation/transition. Such review points are usually identified at programme start-up and should be identified in the programme management plan. Such reviews are time-consuming, and thus adequate budgets and resources should be provided for the programme management team to prepare for them. These reviews may take the form of 'gateways' where a formal go/no-go decision is taken about the subsequent activity.

Review and update programme plans

The programme plan and consolidated schedule are likely to need regular updates as a result of:

- activities that were known to be required, such as the initiation of a new project, but which could not be planned in detail at the start of the tranche;
- changes to the plans and schedules of existing projects as a result of delay or unexpected problems and difficulties;
- alterations to the scope, content or composition of the programme as a result of change requests.

Major updates should be discussed with and agreed by the programme board.

Confirm business case viability

The programme business case is a 'living' document through the life of the programme. It will be consulted and reviewed (a) in the event of changes to the programme or the environment around the programme, or (b) in the event of revised expected benefits and costs arising as greater certainty is gained or benefits are reviewed. At the very least it is always reviewed at the end of each tranche to confirm the on-going viability of the programme. If the business case diverges significantly from the expected return from the programme then the senior responsible owner should recommend programme termination to the senior management team (sponsoring group).

ii Transition

Plan, undertake and confirm transition

The transition from programme outcomes to changes in the day-to-day business or environment requires careful planning prior to the end of each tranche. Areas such as staff training, support arrangements, new processes and their performance measurement, organisational changes and detailing any new data requirements all have to be considered, and especially how these will be introduced with minimum disruption to the business. The transition itself can only be triggered when all areas are ready, and the preparation and management of the transition is a key element of the responsibilities of the business change managers in the programme.

Once the outcomes have been achieved in the organisational environment then the changes can be made permanent by removing old legacy systems and monitoring the embedding of new practices for any issues arising. Lessons from the transition and the implementation of new capabilities have to be fed back to the programme team (in the case of intermediate transitions to influence ongoing programme activities), and to senior or portfolio management teams (for ongoing business continuous improvement and process optimisation).

iii Benefits realisation

Manage benefits realisation

Whilst the transition activity is a key point in establishing and measuring benefits, benefits realisation management occurs throughout the programme delivery phase. The programme tranches (and hence programme schedule) are built around the intended realisation of intermediate benefits, and the benefits themselves should be the basis for any key programme decisions (possibly using techniques such as multi-criteria decision analysis based around the benefits).

Where it is possible (and planned) initial benefits will be measured during the post-transition activity and results fed back into the programme planning for the next tranche (or potentially future tranches). The results may also have an impact on the viability of the business case.

iv Continuous learning environment

Undertake learning activities throughout the programme

Learning, embedding lessons learnt and undertaking improvements should be continuous activities throughout the life of a programme. There are also key points at which it is important to reflect on past activities and consider what is required to enable future success. These reviews should occur at the end of each project and at the end of each tranche. Lessons should also be fed back into the organisational learning environment to help other current and future programmes.

2.6.4 Relevant *APM Body of Knowledge* sections

The following sections of *APM Body of Knowledge* provide further information on the elements of the delivery phase (other sections of *APM Body of Knowledge* also provide information):

1.1.5 Knowledge management	3.1.1 Business case	3.2.5 Requirements management
2.1.1 Communication	3.1.2 Control	3.2.6 Solutions development
2.1.2 Conflict resolution	3.1.5 Planning	3.3.1 Resource scheduling
2.1.3 Delegation	3.1.6 Stakeholder management	3.3.2 Time scheduling
2.1.4 Influencing	3.2.1 Benefits management	3.4.1 Budgeting and cost control
2.1.5 Leadership	3.2.2 Change control	3.5.1 Risk context
2.1.6 Negotiation	3.2.4 Change management	3.5.2 Risk techniques
2.1.7 Teamwork		

2.7 Programme closure phase

2.7.1 Purpose

The purpose of the closure phase is to undertake all final actions and formally recognise that the programme has completed.

2.7.2 Overview

An overview of the closure phase activities, inputs, outputs, controls and supporting mechanisms is given in Figure 2.9 below.

2.7.3 Key activities

A programme will be closed either if all the outcomes required for the future state in the blueprint have been achieved (noting that the blueprint may be adjusted during the course of the programme), or if the sponsor has proposed

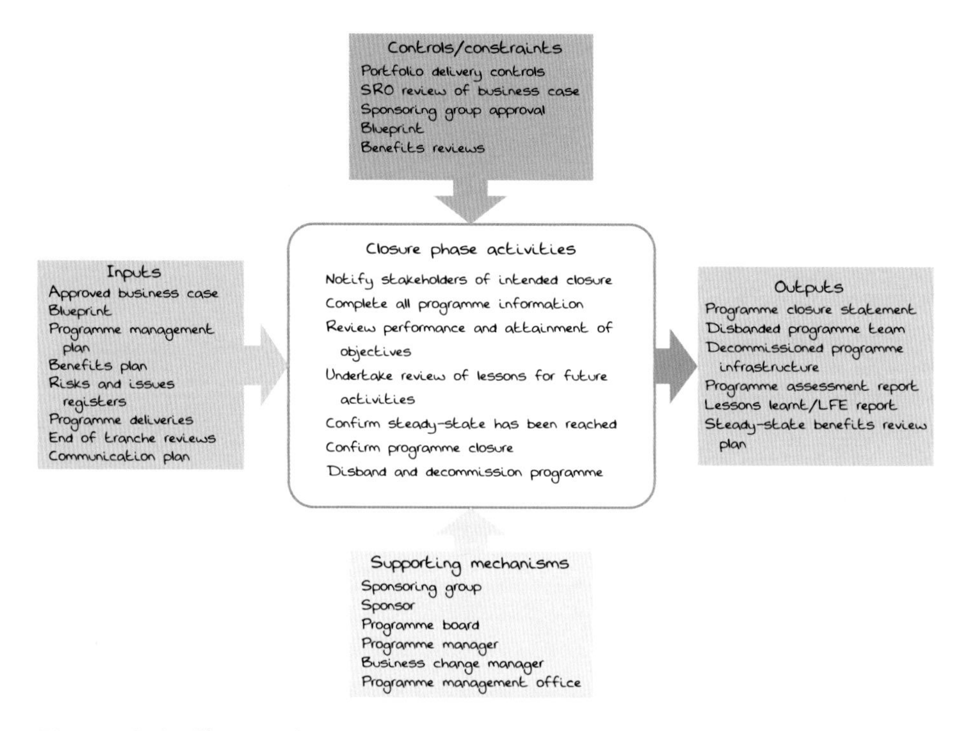

Figure 2.9 Closure phase overview

a premature cessation (for example, based on the business case no longer being viable).

The point at which the closure phase is undertaken, and its duration, will depend upon the nature of the programme. For example, if the outcome of the programme is the operation of a new facility, closure is likely to occur as soon as the last project has completed and the final transition has been undertaken with the facility being handed over to the line management. Alternatively, where the programme is required to achieve a complex range of business benefits, there may need to be a period of use by the customer of the new capabilities before the benefits can start to be realised, or expected to be realised with sufficient confidence. In these circumstances there may need to be a longer period of time between the final transition and the final programme closure activity.

In either case, once the programme enters the closure phase, stakeholders will first be notified that the programme is about to complete, in accordance with the communication plan, and elicit feedback from these stakeholders. The programme team will then ensure that all programme documentation is completed and filed in accordance with the relevant business processes. This activity is often under significant pressure as businesses seek to re-allocate programme teams early as the closure phase is erroneously perceived to add little value, but incomplete or missing records will cause downstream problems, particularly for the new steady-state operations or for any new related programmes.

A review of programme activity and performance will be undertaken. This is an important review, the purpose of which will be to verify, amongst other things, that:

- all deliverables and capabilities have been delivered and transitioned to normal operations successfully;
- all projects have completed their own individual project closures;
- all necessary records are now in place;
- all customer and supplier invoices have been processed;
- lessons have been reviewed and incorporated into corporate activities and processes, and other valuable knowledge, including an up-to-date programme summary, has been captured.

The programme team will then provide a report to the sponsoring group/portfolio delivery group, which will confirm the programme closure. It is recommended that some form of celebration is held to recognise the success of the programme and the efforts of all those involved in the programme, and that this occurs before the programme team is fully redeployed back into the organisation.

2.7.4 Relevant *APM Body of Knowledge* sections

The following sections of the *APM Body of Knowledge* provide further information on the elements of the closure phase (other sections of *APM Body of Knowledge* also provide information):

1.1.5 Knowledge management	2.1.5 Leadership	3.3.1 Resource scheduling
1.2.2 Operations management	3.1.6 Stakeholder management	3.4.2 Funding
1.2.3 Strategic management	3.2.5 Requirements management	3.6.2 Reviews

3

Programme assessment

3.1 Models

Thus far we have described what a programme is and its life cycle; in this section, we offer a range of conceptual models that allow a programme to be assessed through a range of lenses to establish the level of confidence that a programme will be successful. A number of models, or structures, are available and this guide selects illustrative examples with no implied endorsement:

- Body of knowledge.
- Programme framework health checks.
- Assessment models.

3.1.1 Body of knowledge

A body of knowledge, such as *APM Body of Knowledge* or PMI's *PMBOK®*, structures knowledge in a manner that allows portfolios, programmes and projects, or rather the skills required to deliver them, to be assessed. As an example, *APM Body of Knowledge* describes, under the headings of context, people, delivery and interfaces, the complete set of concepts, terms and activities that make up our professional domain. The major shortcoming of using this as a framework to review a programme is the 53 separate topics of knowledge and the absence of an established assessment structure. Both these could be addressed if no better model is available.

3.1.2 Frameworks: Managing Successful Programmes (MSP®)[24]/Agile Programme Management (AgilePM®)[25]

MSP® and AgilePM® are probably the two best-known methodologies for delivery of major programmes. Both have some guiding principles that provide a

[24] MSP Handbook from AXELOS https://www.axelos.com/store/book/managing-successful-programmes. MSP® is a registered trade mark of AXELOS Limited. All rights reserved.
[25] For more on the DSDM Consortium's AgilePM® see http://agileprogrammemanager.com/

health check for a programme being delivered using their methodology. These frameworks are particularly strong on the 'soft skills' – leadership and 'visioning'. The seven principles in MSP® are:

1. Remaining aligned with corporate strategy.
2. Learning from experience.
3. Designing and delivering a coherent capability.
4. Adding value.
5. Focusing on the benefits and threats to them.
6. Envisioning and communicating a better future.
7. Leading change.

The agile philosophy that "an agile programme delivers what is required when it is required – no more no less" is a sound approach for all programmes and is backed by five principles to direct the attitude of those involved.

1. Continuous goal alignment to business strategy.
2. Early and incremental benefits realisation.
3. Governance focused on creating coherent capability.
4. Decision making delegated to lowest possible level.
5. Agile programmes are iterative and may contain agile and non-agile projects.

The two sets of principles show considerable overlap and all should strike a chord with anyone involved in programme management. However, while both afford guidance to staff in programmes, neither provides a suitable structure for this guide to give a reflective assessment of capabilities required for programme success.

3.1.3 Assessment models: P3M3®/programme assessment matrices

In 2000, in response to the poor performance of Government projects and programmes, the Office of Government Commerce (OGC) was established to improve delivery. OGC developed a number of tools, including gateway reviews, to drive improvement and one of these was a 'methodology agnostic' maturity model: the portfolio, programme and project management maturity model (P3M3®)[26]. Analytical maturity models, such as the initial versions of P3M3®, are often not strong on the soft skills relating to leadership and the 'visionary' aspects of managing a programme (although version 3 of P3M3®, launched in 2015, introduced cross-cutting Threads within the full analysis approach to help address this issue). But P3M3® does have the benefit of taking a consistent approach to its chosen seven Perspectives[27] across portfolio, programme and project management and thereby allow the differences to be highlighted. Furthermore, the model can be run as a self-assessment or externally assessed and provides a progressive way of reviewing the maturity of any portfolio, programme or project in a highly repeatable manner. Since the release of P3M3® Version 3, access to P3M3® is primarily through AXELOS Accredited Consultancy Organisations or the substantial self-assessment at commercial rates. While the basic self-assessment is simplistic, it does offer an established, structured, reflective approach.

A range of other assessment matrices exist, such as the one developed in 2011/12 as a research project at Cranfield School of Management.[28] This work developed six progressive, linked three-by-three matrices to ask simple questions around technology, business and people aspects in order to assess the confidence of programme success. The result proved useful to the 10 organisations taking part in the research and is widely available.

Given the 'methodology agnostic' and maturity model concept of P3M3® that allows application to organisations as well as discrete programmes, this guide will use P3M3® as its model to guide the reader through a reflective assessment of some key considerations in the successful delivery of a programme. The operation of the maturity model[29] will not be described here but the seven Perspectives will be explained as they apply at programme level, in order to help the reader to look at their own programmes and organisation through these lenses. Given the generic nature of OGC's work, a conscious decision was taken NOT to cover the 'technical' aspects (engineering, medicine, business change etc.) of programmes and projects. The rationale is that these (clearly) differ very widely depending on the nature of the business; the seven Perspectives are considered to have widespread application to projects and programmes of all natures and using any methodology.

[26] P3M3® is now run by AXELOS, a private sector joint venture between Capita and the Cabinet Office.

[27] Refer to Section 3.1.2.

[28] See http://www.som.cranfield.ac.uk/som/dinamic-content/media/Programme%20Assessment%20Matrices.pdf

[29] For this, refer to the AXELOS website – https://www.axelos.com/best-practice-solutions/p3m3

3.2 Organisational governance

The first perspective views the programme from the 'outside looking in' and seeks to ensure that effective structures (internal and external) are established to provide strong and effective oversight, challenge and direction supported by independent assurance to ensure efficient and timely decision making. Too often 'efficient and timely' decision making is compromised by onerous governance and assurance by entities that hold authority without accountability and feel no personal ownership of programme success. This perspective can be considered to have four interconnected dimensions: governance (including the approvals regime) of the programme; assurance of programme products; design of the operating model for the programme; and the role, responsibilities, authorities and accountabilities (R2A2) for each role in the organisation – which need to flow coherently from the delegations in the governance regime. Given that programmes are about realising benefit from projects in business-as-usual activities, there is a natural tension between an organisation optimised for delivery of projects and one designed for delivering business-as-usual. Furthermore, the complex relationship between programme sponsor or SRO, project sponsors, programme manager and project managers (see also Figure 3.3) is an area frequently not well understood without clear R2A2.

3.2.1 Governance

This aspect addresses how the programme is set up (rather than the management organisation), ensures that delegations to and empowerment of the programme management organisation is sufficient to enable them to deliver, and establishes the mechanisms through which approvals at programme and project levels are delivered. (APM's *Directing Change: A Guide to Governance of Project Management*[30] is recommended reading here). Of particular importance at programme level is the relationship between programme delivery and the business-as-usual team who will use the outputs of the component projects to realise programme benefits within routine operations for the business.

[30] See APM publications, https://www.apm.org.uk/DirectingChange

3.2.2 Assurance

Assurance[31] is the means by which decision makers gain confidence that the propositions coming from the programme are sound. 'Good' assurance requires assurance bodies to be independent of the programme while being actively involved in providing progressive assurance (rather than parachuting in for specific events) and working in a way that support programme success rather than requiring 'further work' that does not materially change programme products. Assurance of any particular aspect of the programme should happen once only and be undertaken by the appropriate 'expert'. Further assurance should satisfy itself as to the competence of and techniques deployed by the assurer rather than subjecting the target to double jeopardy.

3.2.3 Organisation

Drawing a 'wiring diagram' is straightforward; what is less easy is the structured analysis required to identify the functions and services required by the programme, how they should interact and what the optimum balance is between 'project' and 'functional' relationships and between the programme team and business-as-usual elements of the organisation. Key to this is the appreciation that a wiring diagram can only portray a simple two-dimensional line management relationship; in programme delivery, few individuals have exclusive accountability to one individual for all their responsibilities. Whilst the clarity provided by a wiring diagram is necessary, it is not sufficient: and this is where a comprehensive set of R2A2 adds value.

3.2.4 Role, responsibilities, authority and accountabilities (R2A2)

Most people and organisations are very familiar with a job description that sets out the role and responsibilities for the post concerned. In the more complex world of programme management, clarity comes with understanding what authority has been delegated to whom. This authority is limited by the governance structure set up for the programme and should not be hard wired to a post as the delegation should be a subjective judgement made by the

[31] HMG's guidance on assurance is available at https://www.gov.uk/government/publications/major-projects-approval-and-assurance-guidance

organisation based on the confidence they have in the individual's competence and reliability. Too often the 'accountability' aspect of R2A2 is confused with the RACI meaning of accountability; in RACI, accountability refers to the individual held to account for the activity being described even though that individual may delegate responsibility for executing the work to another party (as named in the RACI matrix). In R2A2, being focused on the role rather than the activity, accountability refers to the individual/post to whom this role is accountable for discharging specific aspects of their responsibilities. Frequently, the role will be accountable to different posts for different aspects of their responsibilities. The simplest example is the project manager, who is accountable to the project sponsor for the outputs of the project and to the programme manager for the coherence of the project with other aspects of the programme. (See Section 3.6.1 below.)

3.3 Management control

The second perspective views the programme 'from the inside' and sets up the control and reporting mechanisms for the programme. At the heart of this lies the programme management office (PMO) which can be a 'thick' or a 'thin' layer depending on: the nature of the programme; decisions on governance; the closeness of interrelationship between the constituent projects; and the degree of central services and control provided to, and exercised over, day to day operations. Much has been written on this topic and this guide draws the reader's attention to other APM publications such as *Planning, Scheduling, Monitoring and Control*[32] for further information. One aspect that does demand mention here is the imperative for management control at the programme level to retain a systems thinking outlook. It is very easy for management control to dive into the detailed supervision of project activities and miss the true value adding aspects of the 'whole system, whole life' perspective. The well-proven technique of earned value management (EVM)[33] should be applied at project level and used at programme level to understand potential impacts across the programme and, thereby, to drive programme level decision making.

[32] Published in 2015 and available at https://www.apm.org.uk/Planning-Monitoring-Scheduling-Control

[33] See APM publications, https://www.apm.org.uk/EarnedValueManagement

3.4 Benefits management

Where projects are about delivering 'outputs', programmes are about delivering 'outcomes' and the benefits associated with incorporating the outcomes in business-as-usual activities. In this respect, most programmes involve a 'business change' or 'transition' component above and beyond the delivery of the project output. Benefits management at programme level can be particularly challenging as:

- there can be a very heavy reliance on customers and users (both their behaviour and their feedback);
- the benefits are often in a form that is neither easy to measure nor in the vested interest of some stakeholders to achieve;
- there is frequently a long lead time between project outputs and benefits realisation during which time the baseline has moved or other factors have impacted the outcome;
- the comparison is between 'what is' and 'what would have been' with some parties having a vested interest in shaping the 'would have been' and others taking the view that 'what might have been' is no longer relevant as we have to live in the 'world as we find it';
- business cases are prone to over-statement of benefits in order to gain approval.

Benefits management is often misunderstood or misinterpreted but it is a vitally important change management function that demands excellent communications, a robust process and sustained support from all change stakeholders during implementation across the project and programme management business landscape so that the true impact of cost, operational, organisation and/or compliance-based benefits can be measured and realised. Various APM white papers[34] have been produced to aid people trying to develop their understanding and skill in this area: pick the one most relevant to your needs.

[34] Given the dynamic nature of this topic, the APM Benefits SIG has opted to develop a series of focused white papers rather than a single comprehensive guide. The white papers can be found on the APM website at https://www.apm.org.uk/white-papers

3.5 Stakeholder management

Good stakeholder management in the programme arena requires the same skills as good stakeholder management in other walks of life, using tools relevant to the scale of the task – ranging from a simple two-by-two importance-by-influence matrix to sophisticated stakeholder relationship management software. While categorisation of stakeholders into: client/sponsor, user, customer, supplier, influencer, beneficiaries, team/staff, etc, will always apply, the principal challenges for stakeholder management at programme level often arise in three areas discussed below.

3.5.1 Intra programme

As described in Section 3.1, the relationship between sponsor teams and delivery teams at programme and project levels within the programme requires careful stakeholder management to ensure that project drivers and incentives do not drive sub-optimal programme consequences. This is a greater risk where the client/sponsor organisation is not experienced at programme management and hence sponsor/SRO relationships are not mature. Getting the relationships right

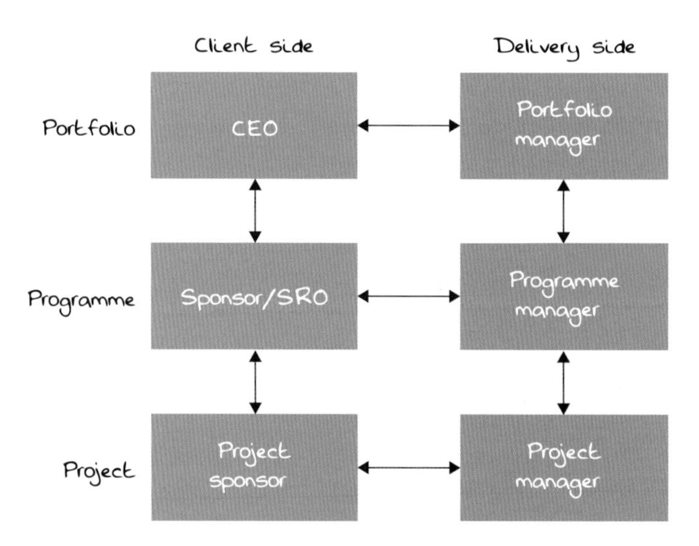

Figure 3.1 Key stakeholder relationships between projects, programmes and portfolios

between the 'corners of the square' can be a real challenge and all parties should resist the temptation to have conversations across the diagonals as this cuts across the correct governance relationships.

3.5.2 Business-as-usual stakeholders

In a highly tuned business focused on business-as-usual activity and unfamiliar with programmes and projects, the challenges of managing business-as-usual stakeholders can be twofold. First, the organisational design (see Section 3.2.3) of business-as-usual is frequently at odds with programme and project R2A2 (see Section 3.2.4), which cut across functional hierarchies. Second, at programme level it is usually the business-as-usual stakeholders (the target audience for the business change projects within the programme) who will be expected to adapt their way of working if the benefits of the programme are to be realised. People will have a mix of responses to the changes, some being more enthusiastic than others, and many having real concerns that it will be important to surface, consider and respond to. Any points on Elisabeth Kübler-Ross's change curve[35] would be good starting positions to understand the different emotions that people might be experiencing.

3.5.3 External to programme

The larger and more high profile the programme, the greater the number of 'experts' in the topic who believe they have a critical and legitimate interest in it – usually from a narrow viewpoint and often with very little understanding of the basic principles of programme management. Most will believe they are able to wield a 'red card' – which is why setting up the governance (Section 3.2) correctly is a prerequisite for successful programme delivery. However, the power of 'influence' should never be underestimated and streamlined governance alone is not sufficient to manage the key external stakeholders: this takes time, effort and a full appreciation that 'communications' is two-way process. The importance of building 'public' support for the programme (and the role of the media, including social media, at the appropriate level – national, regional, neighbourhood, company-wide or at divisional level) should not be underestimated: nor should the steps that the 'nay-sayers' may be willing to take to undermine the programme.

[35] Kübler-Ross, E. (1969) *On Death and Dying*, Routledge, ISBN 0-415-04015-9.

3.6 Risk management

At every point during a programme, there will be uncertain events or situations that could affect the direction of the programme, the achievement of desired outcomes or the realisation of expected benefits. These uncertain events or situations, and their consequences, are the risks that the programme must manage and relate to the role of programme management in providing the link between individual projects and their strategic intent. Programmes are fundamentally different from projects; as a result, risks at programme level should be viewed differently from those at project level. The description of risk management here deliberately goes into proportionately greater detail than for the other Perspectives in this section in light of the significance of risk management at this level.

Using projects as the fundamental delivery mechanism, Figure 3.1 shows the structural relationship that links programmes and projects within the organisational environment and provides a framework to deliver beneficial change to organisations via programmes, by transferring strategy down, whilst delivering capability up. It is this organisational environment and the relationship between programmes, projects and strategy that underpin how risks are viewed at programme level. Major change is usually synonymous with complexity, risk, many interdependencies to manage and conflicting priorities to resolve. By employing a tailored approach to risk management within the programme environment, practitioners will be better equipped to tackle increased complexity and, although the established concepts of project risk management practice may be applied, the application of these tools may need to be different.

But how does the programme manager relate the 'traditional' project risk management methodologies and tools, within the context of programme risk management? To help answer this we first need to understand the sources of risk from a programme perspective; Figure 3.2 highlights potential sources.

Although there are close similarities between the process for explicit management of individual programme risks and the well-established project risk management process, programme risks can arise from above and below the programme (within the organisational context) as well as from within it and, therefore, the programme risk management process must tackle all of these sources.

In summary, risks driving uncertainty within programmes originate from:

- strategic level;
- project level;

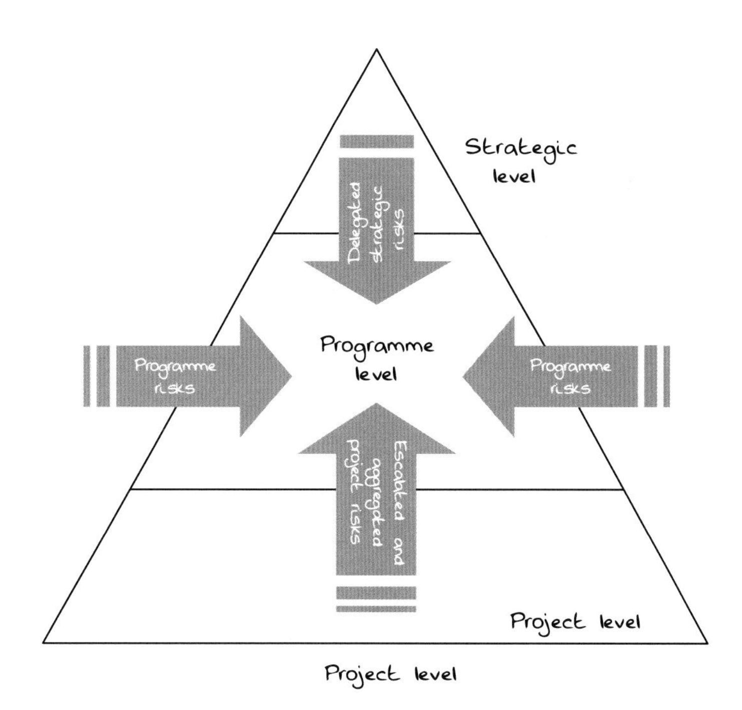

Figure 3.2 Sources of programme risk (reproduced from Hillson, 2009[36])

- within the programme (derived from interfaces between programme components and external risks termed EXPLICIT risks);
- programme risks originating from actual programme execution termed IMPLICIT risks;
- non-project components.

The main risk treatment processes and their sources are:

- aggregation – project to programme;
- escalation – project to programme;
- delegation – strategic level to programme;
- assimilation – from within the programme including explicit and implicit risks.

We now extend Figure 3.2 to overlay risk treatment processes on the programme risk sources to see a suggested methodology for managing programme risk

[36] See Hillson, D. A. 2009. *Managing Risk in Projects*. Farnham, UK: Gower. ISBN 978-0-566-08867.

(Figure 3.3). Much has been written on this topic and this guide draws the reader's attention to other publications such as AXELOS's 'Management of Risk'[37]

It is recognised that in project risk management, the focus is on managing threats and opportunities to the delivery of project outputs. Given the focus of programmes is on delivering benefits, programme managers are likely to focus on events that threaten benefits realisation and the programmes ability to deliver change management activities within the programme as well as the combined impact of the project risk and risks delegated from portfolio or strategic level.

A critical component of programme-level risk management lies in the establishment, estimating and release (either to relevant projects or back to funders) of risk funding. Human nature dictates that 'project money will usually get spent' – if

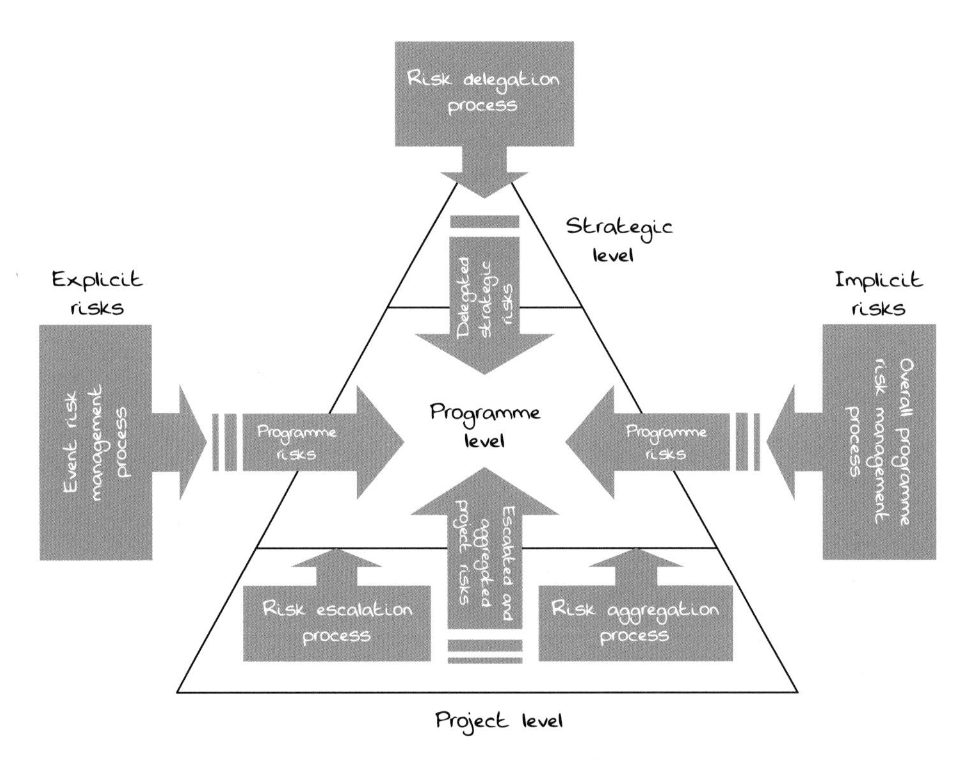

Figure 3.3 Programme risk sources, mechanisms and treatment processes

[37] See OGC's Management of Risk (https://www.axelos.com/store/book/management-of-risk-guidance-for-practitioners) and/or APM's *Project Risk Analysis Management Guide* (https://www.apm.org.uk/PRAMGuide).

it is not used to mitigate threats it might be utilised to deliver additional scope requested by the client; irrespective of whether this represents best value for money at higher levels. 'Good practice' at programme level will see the programme manager controlling the release of project risk funding to project managers using appropriate change control with risk provision held at various levels and released accordingly. A particular benefit of this approach is that the whole programme risk provision should be considerably less than the sum of all project risk provisions. Furthermore, any unrequired provision can be released to the portfolio manager or client progressively for reinvestment in the business, rather than being hoarded until the 'last safe moment' when the project comes in under budget – to the delight of some and the frustration of others.

3.7 Financial management

While this topic recognises the needs of good financial accounting, the differentiator here lies in getting the financial accountants to recognise and embrace the needs of project accounting. Programme finances do not follow the normal predictable cycle (very often annual) of business accounts and gaining recognition that whilst programmes can (and must) deliver annual accounts, optimum performance is not achieved by constraining programmes through strict annual metrics. In this respect, a material contribution that the programme management team will make is managing the financial approval cycle for the business on behalf of the constituent projects in the programme.

Whilst the approval structure is established under organisational governance (Section 3.2) and the benefits realised through benefits management (Section 3.4), the business case itself is developed, managed and tracked under the financial management function. When change occurs – as it does on every programme – a change impact assessment is required to validate the impact on the business case and take action accordingly.

One of the key roles of financial management at programme level is setting and delivering the optimal structure for risk and contingency budgets across the programme. The naturally conservative nature of good project managers indicates that they will seek (and retain) a larger risk and contingency budget than they are likely to require: good programme management needs to strike the right balance and ensure that the money set aside for risk and contingency is assessed across the programme so that it can be released – to projects or back to funders – in a way that avoids tying up capital in an inefficient manner for the business as a whole. Few will applaud a programme manager who hands back a large lump sum of unused contingency at the very end of the programme.

3.8 Resource management

The seventh perspective is widely acknowledged to have four components.

3.8.1 Human resources

The first and most widely recognised component is the P3M staff involved in the enterprise, including their competence and training. At programme level, this is very much about ensuring that the right staff with the right skills are available and appropriately balanced across the PMO and component projects. Where the programme exists within an enduring organisation, staff development for the future and succession planning within the programme and at portfolio level are important considerations.

3.8.2 Supply chain

Few commercial/procurement staff appreciate being 'subordinated' to the second level of the Perspectives model but, within this conceptual framework, the supply chain (and the resources and material it brings) is but one – often dominant in financial and delivery terms – aspect of resource management. At programme level, supply chain management is frequently critical as most contracts are let at project level, but optimal programme delivery requires coordination of delivery (or resource deployment) at programme or even portfolio level to ensure efficient use of such resources across the whole programme.

3.8.3 Infrastructure

The physical and virtual infrastructure for the programme (and the projects within it) is a critical resource that requires careful consideration during programme set up at the beginning of the delivery phase of the life cycle. This is the bedrock on which effective management control is built and demands careful thought in terms of integration across projects and into business-as-usual (both during programme delivery and once incorporated into business-as-usual).

3.8.4 Information

Information in a programme is a key resource and demands careful consideration of its structuring and treatment – as with infrastructure, effort committed to this early in the life cycle is seldom wasted. To be clear, the information resource is an 'enabler': it needs to be managed within the IT infrastructure and 'used' within other relevant Perspectives. But unless it is structured correctly from the outset (using principles such as 'one version of the truth'), communicated and followed with discipline, programme execution will be inefficient and record keeping may be inadequate. Even where a programme may not be large enough to justify the formal appointment of a chief information officer, the role should be allocated to someone with the competence and authority to exercise control in this key area.

3.9 Summary

The use of conceptual frameworks to 'look at' a programme allows a reflective analysis of performance and delivery confidence. Covering all the Perspectives outlined here is no guarantee of programme success – but poor coverage of any of the topics will materially increase the likelihood of failure.

Glossary

Agile A family of development methodologies where requirements and solutions are developed iteratively and incrementally throughout the life cycle.

Benefit The quantifiable and measurable improvement resulting from completion of deliverables that is perceived as positive by a stakeholder. It will normally have a tangible value, expressed in monetary terms that will justify the investment.

Benefits management The identification, definition, planning, tracking and realisation of business benefits.

Benefits realisation The practice of ensuring that benefits are derived from outputs and outcomes.

Blueprint A document defining and describing what a programme is designed to achieve in terms of the business and operational vision.

Board A body that provides sponsorship to a programme. The board will represent financial, provider and user interests.

Brief The output of the concept phase of a programme.

Business-as-usual An organisation's normal, day-to-day operations.

Business case Provides justification for undertaking a programme. It evaluates the benefit, cost and risk of alternative options and provides a rationale for the preferred solution.

Business change manager The role responsible for benefits management from identification through to realisation.

Change control The process through which all requests to change the baseline scope of a programme are captured, evaluated and then approved, rejected or deferred.

Change management A structured approach to moving an organisation from the current state to the desired future state.

Closure The formal end point of a programme, either because it has been completed or because it has been terminated early.

Competence framework A set of competences and competencies that may be used to define a role.

Concept The first phase in the programme life cycle. During this phase the need, opportunity or problem is confirmed, the overall feasibility of the work is considered and a preferred solution identified.

Configuration management The administrative activities concerned with the creation, maintenance, controlled change and quality control of the programme scope.

Contingency Resource set aside for responding to unidentified risks.

Control Tracking performance against agreed plans and taking corrective action required to meet defined objectives.

Definition The second phase of a programme life cycle where requirements are refined and the preferred solution, and ways of achieving it, are identified.

Disbenefit A consequence of change perceived as negative by one or more stakeholders.

Environment The circumstances and conditions within which the programme must operate.

Financial management The process of estimating and justifying costs in order to secure funds, controlling expenditure and evaluating outcomes.

Gate The point between phases, gates and/or tranches where a go/no-go decision can be made about the remainder of the work.

Governance The set of policies, regulations, functions, processes, procedures and responsibilities that define the establishment, management and control programmes.

Handover The point in the life cycle where deliverables are handed over to the sponsor and users.

Information management The collection, storage, dissemination, archiving and destruction of information. It enables teams and stakeholders to use their time, resource and expertise effectively to make decisions and to fulfil their roles.

Issue A formal issue occurs when the tolerances of delegated work are predicted to be exceeded or have been exceeded. This triggers the escalation of the issue from one level of management to the next in order to seek a solution.

Leadership The ability to establish vision and direction, to influence and align others towards a common purpose and to empower and inspire people to achieve success.

Lessons learned Documented experiences that can be used to improve the future management of programmes.

Life cycle The inter-related phases of a programme, providing a structure for governing the progression of work.

Mandate The mandate is used to enable the sponsoring group to decide whether to allocate resources to fully explore the potential for a programme.

Management plan A plan that sets out the policies and principles that will be applied to the management of some aspects of the programme. Examples include a risk management plan, a communication management plan and a quality management plan.

Maturity model An organisational model that describes a number of evolutionary stages through which an organisation improves its management process.

Objectives Predetermined results towards which effort is directed. Objectives may be defined in terms of outputs, outcomes and/or benefits.

Opportunity A positive risk event that, if it occurs, will have a beneficial effect on achievement of objectives.

Optimising The fifth and last level of a typical maturity model where continuous process improvement is enabled by quantitative feedback from the process and from piloting innovative ideas and technologies.

Organisation The management structure applicable to the programme and the organisational environment in which it operates.

Outcome The changed circumstances or behaviour that results from the use of an output.

Output The tangible or intangible product typically delivered by a project.

Phase The major sub-division of a life cycle.

Portfolio A grouping of an organisation's projects and programmes. Portfolios can be managed at an organisational or functional level.

Product A tangible or intangible component of a project's output synonymous with deliverable.

Programme A group of related projects and change management activities that together achieve beneficial change for an organisation.

Programme management The coordinated management of projects and change management activities to achieve beneficial change.

Project A unique, transient endeavour undertaken to achieve planned objectives.

Quality The fitness for purpose or the degree of confidence of the outputs, benefits and the processes by which they are delivered, meet stakeholder requirements and are fit for purpose.

Requirements management The process of capturing, assessing and justifying stakeholder's wants and needs.

Resource management The acquisition and deployment of the internal and external resources required to deliver the programme.

Resources All those items required to undertake work including people, finance and materials.

Risk The potential of an action or event to impact on the achievement of objectives.

Risk analysis An assessment and synthesis of risk events to gain an understanding of their individual significance and their combined impact on objectives.

Risk event An uncertain event or set of circumstances that would, if it occurred, have an effect on the achievement of one or more objectives.

Risk management A process that allows individual risk events and overall risk to be understood and managed proactively, optimising success by minimising threats and maximising opportunities.

Risk register A document listing identified risk events and their corresponding planned responses.

Schedule A timetable showing the forecast start and finish dates for activities or events within a programme.

Scope The totality of the outputs, outcomes and benefits and the work required to produce them.

Scope management The process whereby outputs, outcomes and benefits are identified, defined and controlled.

Setting The relationship of the programme with its host organisation.

Sponsorship An important senior management role. The sponsor is accountable for ensuring that the work is governed effectively and delivers the objectives that meet identified needs.

Stakeholder The organisations or people who have an interest or role in the programme or are impacted by it.

Stakeholder management The systematic identification, analysis, planning and implication of actions designed to engage stakeholders.

Threat A negative risk event; a risk event that if it occurs will have a detrimental effect on the objectives.

Tranche A sub-division of the delivery phase of a programme created to facilitate approval gates at suitable points in the life cycle.

Users The group of people who are intended to receive benefits or operate outputs.

Vision The vision describes the future state the programme is intended to deliver.

Vee Model A sequential life cycle model used to represent the continuous verification and validation of plans and results.

References

APM EVM SIG (2008), *Earned Value Management: APM Guidelines, 2nd edition*. Princes Risborough, Association for Project Management.

APM Governance SIG (2011), *Directing Change: A Guide to the Governance of Project Management*. Princes Risborough, Association for Project Management.

APM North West branch (2015), *The Practical Adoption of Agile Methodologies*. Available at https://www.apm.org.uk/sites/default/files/The-Practical-Adoption-of-Agile-Methodologies.pdf

APM PMC SIG (2015), *Planning, Scheduling, Monitoring and Control: The Practical Project Management of Time, Cost and Risk*. Princes Risborough, Association for Project Management.

APM PMO SIG (n.d.). Available at https://www.apm.org.uk/group/apm-pmo-specific-interest-group

APM Risk SIG (2010), *Project Risk Analysis and Management Guide, 2nd edition*. Princes Risborough, Association for Project Management.

Association for Project Management (2007), *Models to Improve the Management of Projects*. Princes Risborough, Association for Project Management.

Association for Project Management (2012), *APM Body of Knowledge 6th edition*. Princes Risborough, Association for Project Management.

Association for Project Management (2015), *APM Competence Framework, 2nd edition*. Princes Risborough. Available at https://www.apm.org.uk/competence-framework

AXELOS (2010), *Management of Risk Guidance for Practitioners, London*.

AXELOS (2011), *Managing Successful Programmes, London*.

AXELOS (2015), *Portfolio, Programme and Project Management Maturity Model (P3M3), London*.

Gray, A. and Richardson, K. (2015), *Valuing Our Place in the World – Using Systems Engineering in Programme and Project Management*, INCOSE UK Annual Systems Engineering Conference.

Hillson, D. A. (2009), *Managing Risk in Projects*. Farnham.

References

HM Treasury (2015), *Public Sector Business Cases Using the 5 Case Model* (HM Treasury Green Book supplementary guidance). Available at https://www.gov.uk/government/publications/the-green-book-appraisal-and-evaluation-in-central-governent [sic].

Kübler-Ross, E. (1969), *On Death and Dying*. Routledge.

Index

Index